IRISH ROCK

WHERE IT'S COME FROM
WHERE IT'S AT
WHERE IT'S GOING

GILL AND MACMILLAN

IRISH ROCK

WHERE IT'S COME FROM
WHERE IT'S AT
WHERE IT'S GOING

Published in Ireland by
Gill and Macmillan Ltd
Goldenbridge
Dublin 8
with associated companies in
Auckland, Budapest, Gaborone, Harare, Hong Kong,
Kampala, Kuala Lumpur, Lagos, London, Madras,
Manzini, Melbourne, Mexico City, Nairobi,
New York, Singapore, Sydney, Tokyo, Windhoek
© Copyright 1992 Brown Packaging Limited, 257 Liverpool Road, London N1 1LX
ISBN 0-7171-1997-1
Print origination by Hong Kong Reprohouse Co. Ltd

A catalogue record is available for this book from the British Library.

Printed and bound in Great Britain by BPCC Hazell Books,
Aylesbury, Bucks., England
Member of BPCC Limited

ACKNOWLEDGEMENTS

I'd like to thank the people who have been instrumental in the making of this book: My mother, brother and in-laws for their constant support; Niall Stokes, Editor of *Hot Press*, for publishing my first article in the early 1980s, and his support for hundreds more; Ciaran Carty, Arts Editor, *The Sunday Tribune*, for his unwavering assistance; Terry Hooley; Philip King; George Byrne (for answering a question or three); Davy Carton of The Saw Doctors; Pierce Turner; Gavin Friday; Kieran Owens; Garvan Gallagher; publicist Eveleen Coyle and her assistants Helen Peakin and Monica McInerney for their help with planning and publicity; Sidgwick & Jackson for their belief in the project; and to Graham McColl at Brown Packaging for his editorial assistance.

Finally, this book is dedicated to my wife Angela, whose help in the suggestion department and the proof-reading of various chapters of the book was invaluable. Thank you. Very finally, to my son Paul: may you always know the spiritual and transcendental power of rock music and may you sigh in the face of those who don't.

Tony Clayton-Lea

My mother – for lending me the money to buy my first typewriter
Ferdia MacAnna – for publishing my first article in *In Dublin*
Joe Breen, Maureen Gillespie and Colm McGinty – for early help and encouragement
John George Byrne – for nearly answering the 20 questions
Pat Egan – for the scrapbooks and the reminiscences
Brush, Guru Weirdbrain, Setanta, Simon and Clint – for the verbals
Jackie Hayden – for the green light and the lunches
Thanks also to *The Sunday Press*, Eveleen Coyle and Monica McInerney, Sidgwick & Jackson, Brown Packaging, Johnny Lappin, Freebird Records, and not forgetting The Gravediggers, The Rhythm Kings and the (original) Wilf Brothers.

This book is dedicated with love to my wife Sandra and the two Christophers.

Richie Taylor

Both authors would like to thank the following publications for the extensive use of quotations: *GQ* magazine; *Hot Press* magazine; *In Dublin* magazine; *The Sunday Press*.

PICTURE ACKNOWLEDGEMENTS

A & M Records Ltd: 98/9. The Bees Knees Recording Company Ltd: 40. BMG Enterprises/RCA Victor: 86; 107 (centre left and centre right). Michael Boran: 67. Wally Cassidy: 62. Decoy Records: 126 (right). Kevin Dunne: 42. Ensign Records: 106 (left); 117; 125 (bottom right). Colm Henry: 29. Terry Hooley: 28; 36. Island Records: 21; 54/5. Anton Corbijn: 58. Amelia Stein: 92; 125 (top). Kitchenware Records: 110. Liquid Records: 66; 112. London Features International Ltd: 13; 14/15; 17. Peter Mazcz: 37 (top). Paul Cox: 38/9; 44. Simon Fowler: 53. Tom Sheehan: 73 (bottom); 79. Frank Griffin: 80. Neil Preston: 85. Kevin Cummins: 94. Julian Barton: 101. Alan McCann: 59. MCA Records: 107 (top); 109 (centre); 123 (top). Mother Records/MCA: 88/9; 90; 104; 109 (top); 111; 122 (top). Phonogram Records Ltd (Ireland): 83; 123 (bottom). Pictorial Press: 11; 32. Knaeps, Belgium. Polydor Ltd: 93; 106 (right). Polygram Records Ltd (Ireland): 78. Redferns: 2/3. Michael Linssen: 10. Fin Costello: 22/3. David Redfern: 26. Peter Cronin: 30/1; 34, 51, 75, 81, 82, 87. Mick Hutson: 47, 49 (top). Suzi Gibbons: 68. S. Gillett: 69. S. Moore. Retna Pictures Ltd: 6/7. Fiona Simon: 33. Steve Double: 37 (bottom); 46. Chris Van de Vooren: 48, 50. Paul Slattery: 49 (bottom). A. Indge: 73 (top). Joe Shutter: 77. Kevin Cummins: 84. A.J. Barratt: 103. Tony Mottram. Rex Features Ltd: 12; 16. Fraser Gray: 18. Stills/A. Berly: 25; 35; 70/1; 74. Richard Pasley. Nigel Rolfe: 61. Setanta Records: 72; 96. Joseph Dilworth: 97. Sire Records: 125 (bottom left). Solid Records: 95. Stephen Street: 100; 102; 119; 120 (centre); 122 (bottom). Sovereign Pictures/MCA: 91. Derek Speirs/Report: 24; 57. Ursula Steiger: 65. Stiff Records: 118. Tara Records: 121; 126 (left). Terry Thorpe: 8; 20. Virgin Records: 115 (top); 120 (top and bottom). Warners: 116. WEA: 108; 109 (bottom); 115 (bottom). Val Wilmer: 41; 52.

Pages 2-3: Guitarist Gary Moore in action.

CONTENTS

ROOTS

'Got a job in a showband/Workin' like a slave/Six nights and every Sunday/C'mon and put me on a wage.'

– SKID ROW, 1970.

IN THE BEGINNING WAS THE SHOWBAND, and they ruled the land. A peculiarly Irish phenomenon, sporting neat hairstyles, and dressed in shiny suits and starched shirts, they featured a minimum of seven band members on stage. Non-stop cover versions were churned out with varying degrees of competence.

Throughout the 1960s and most of the 1970s the showbands dominated the live music scene. They played large ballrooms which were either 'wet' or 'dry'. The former had a bar licence, while the latter did not. However, by the mid-1960s there were distinct rumblings in most of the major Irish cities. The beat group phenomenon was about to boom.

Outfits to make an early impact included Bluesville, The Greenbeats, The Chosen Few, The Chessmen, The Semitones, The Movement, The Creatures and The Action, (led, incidentally, by Peter Adler, son of harmonica wizard, Larry).

Dublin was soon spilling over with live beat music, and the action revolved around venues like the Caroline Club, the Crystal Ballroom (now McGonagle's), the Five Club, the Scene Club, and Club a Go Go, as well as an extensive school hall and tennis club circuit in the outer suburbs.

Bluesville, fronted by singer Ian Whitcomb, an American studying at Trinity College, were Dublin's first beat group (strange that it took a visitor to initiate American r'n'b into Ireland). They were performing live in 1964, and soon had hits with 'You Turn Me On' and 'This Sporting Life'. Besides singing, Whitcomb subsequently pursued a career as a producer

LEFT: *Van Morrison and Them on location in London during the mid-1960s.*

7

(most notably Mae West's 'Great Balls Of Fire') and as a novelist and pop chronicler.

Bluesville made their initial recordings in a house on Dublin's Merrion Square after a suggestion from the head of Trinity's drama group that they should record 'something evil and revolutionary'. In his 1983 book **Rock Odyssey,** Whitcomb recalled how they had used a Chuck Berry riff and called the number 'Pall Me Mantle'. In June 1965, 'You Turn Me On' was a Top 10 hit for them in the USA.

Deke O'Brien was a member of Bluesville, and formed Dublin soul band The Chosen Few when Whitcomb took a one-way ticket to the USA. O'Brien was to surface in a variety of bands down through the years, including Bees Make Honey, Nightbus and Stepaside.

However The Greenbeats (a few of whom have performed regularly over the past decade as rock'n'roll/1960s revivalists Full Circle) can also lay claim to initiating Ireland's beat boom. In 1964, they journeyed to Liverpool to play in The Cavern, once the stomping ground of a Liverpudlian quartet called The Beatles.

In Belfast, Van Morrison's Them were one of the most successful groups, while The Gentry from Ballymena and The People (later to become Eire Apparent) from Portadown played on the regular Northern Ireland circuit. Down in Limerick, Granny's Intentions were the main attraction, while over in Cork in 1965 a young Rory Gallagher had temporarily formed his own group in between thankless stints with showbands.

The new beat

While the showbands continued to draw huge crowds in rural areas, and also attracted country people living and working in Dublin city, the beat scene was new and exciting, and regarded as ever so slightly dangerous. These young men, with their loud guitars and primitive rhythms, were labelled 'weird', and many of the clubs attracted the attention of the authorities.

Strabane-born Paul Brady, later to carve out a name for himself in both the Irish traditional and rock fields, actually began his musical career in Dublin beat groups. Attending a city university, he promptly joined a group called The Inmates. He soon fronted his own group called Rockhouse, but was forced to return to his studies, after which he joined ballad group The Johnstons and subsequently embarked on a career in folk/traditional music.

ABOVE: *Pat Egan, a shrewd observer of the Dublin music scene. He has been at the heart of Irish rock music from its beginnings in the 1960s right up to the present day.*

Pat Egan, now a successful agent/promoter/nightclub owner, started hanging around the clubs at the age of 15. 'The Stella in Mount Merrion was the first actual club. I remember seeing Them play there the week that "Baby Please Don't Go" went into the UK charts.'

Indeed, The Stella played host to a countless number of visiting beat groups from the North of Ireland, including The Method, The Few, Soul Foundation and The Gentry. Egan began working as a club disc jockey in 1967 and recalls seeing acclaimed Irish artist Robert Ballagh playing bass with The Chessmen.

Motown comes to Dublin

'I was absolutely brutal at it (disc jockeying), but I used to play trendy things at the time, all the new Motown stuff and that, which was hard to come across. RTE radio had no policy for popular music, except for Ken Stewart's programme.'

He regards the 1960s as an 'Age of Innocence', without any alcohol in the clubs and a pioneering spirit about the music. 'I wish I could do it all over again and keep my eyes open this time around,' he laughs.

'But really, a lot of musicians could have made money if they'd kept their heads.'

Despite their stultifying lack of originality, the showbands proved to be a breeding ground for young talent. Irish guitar hero Rory Gallagher began his career as a member of The Fontana Showband, and the guaranteed income such outfits offered helped many a struggling rock musician out of a tight financial spot.

However, in a 1972 interview with Pat Egan for *New Spotlight* magazine, Thin Lizzy leader Phil Lynott offered a different viewpoint, while recalling how he once nearly accepted a job in a showband: 'At the time I was in two minds about it, but I'm glad I didn't. Showbands have destroyed some of the finest musicians in the country and the guys themselves know it. They come up and actually apologise for being in showbands. Even Eric Bell (then Lizzy guitarist) will tell you it almost drove him crazy playing for two years in The Dreams. Paul Ashford (later to play with south Dublin snob rockers Stepaside and traditional kings The Furey Brothers) was an absolutely fantastic bass player but the bread made him join a showband.'

Skid Row fun

Progressive rockers Skid Row had a reputation for playing louder and faster than anybody else, and their virtuoso-like performances, with Brendan 'Brush' Shiels on bass, Gary Moore on guitar, and Noel 'Nollaig' Bridgeman on drums, were never less than entertaining.

A colourful character, Shiels today recalls this line-up as the best. 'Everything started to fizzle in '71, since then we've just been trying to make a living!'

He began his career with The Uptown Band, and was a member of several other groups before he formed Skid Row. He remembers 1967-1969 as something of a golden age of Irish rock. 'You could be playing seven nights a week, there were plenty of clubs, and none of them served alcohol. It was all new to us.'

Subjects discussed when the groups met in these venues included the new progressive music and the rapidly changing fashion scene. 'I wore flares the first time around, I won't wear them again,' he laughs.

He also remembers the late 1960s as being a time of diverse musical influences, with Irish bands playing everything from soul to progressive rock. Indeed, the first Skid Row single – 'Sandy's Gone' – was in fact a country song. The band were signed by CBS, and released two albums, *Skid* (1970) and *34 Hours* (1971). The former was to show Skid Row as a progressive rock group of some note, by virtue of the album's original material and accomplished performances. The latter was a hurried, almost live, studio album, that suffered from a distinct lack of quality control.

Shiels used to buy second-hand English music magazines in Dublin to catch up on the latest jargon, and claims that he was influenced by 'pseudo-jazz'. After *34 Hours*, Gary Moore departed the line-up (he was to play with several bands, including Thin Lizzy and Colosseum, before his solo career finally took off), and a succession of lead guitarists, including Paul Chapman, Ed Deane, Eric Bell and Jimmy Slevin replaced him.

Ironically enough, by the late 1970s many musicians referred to joining Skid Row as 'signing on the dole' (registering for unemployment benefit). The always straightforward Brush guaranteed them a weekly wage and paid a social welfare stamp, unlike the majority of the other black economy entrepreneurs.

A rock explosion

By 1968, Rory Gallagher was treading the boards with Taste, and an extremely young Phil Lynott was actually lead singer with Skid Row. Rock music was taken seriously as youth culture exploded, and the demarcation lines between pop and rock were drawn. As far as the fans were concerned, bands were either 'progressive' or not, and if not they were beneath contempt. Hair lapped generously over collars, trouser material flared and volume controls were turned up and set for the heart of the sun.

By the late 1960s, psychedelia was rampant, and bands like Dr Strangely Strange, Granny's Intentions, Orange Machine and

> *'I change the programme and the keys of the songs most nights. I never tell any of the boys in the band what I'm going to open up with or anything. They just have to follow me and flutter around a few seconds for the right key. It's the only way you can keep yourself awake some nights'*
>
> – BRUSH SHIELS.

ROOTS

Eire Apparent (featuring guitarist Henry McCullough, later to play with both Sweeney's Men and Paul McCartney's Wings), were all dabbling in the then fashionable milieu of acid rock.

However Rory Gallagher stuck steadfastedly to his rhythm and blues roots, and with Taste churned out hard-nosed rock, while proving himself to be a guitar player *par excellence*. Taste concerts were sweaty celebrations of primal release, where denim-clad fans played the traditional 'air' guitars while frantically shaking their manes, accompanying Gallagher's experienced and superb use of the fretboard.

In 1970, Taste disbanded in what appeared to be acrimonious circumstances. While Gallagher refused to squabble in public, he did admit that: 'John Wilson, Richie McCracken and I were at a complete end not only musically but also as a group of people'. Gallagher set about launching a solo career, which has endured varying levels of success up to the present day.

After spells playing with both The Black Eagles and with Skid Row, in 1970 Phil Lynott formed the first incarnation of Thin Lizzy. It featured Lynott on vocals and on the bass guitar (an instrument that he had been taught to play by Brush Shiels), Brian Downey on drums, Eric Bell on guitar and Eric Wricksen on keyboards. It was to prove a long and eventful musical odyssey for Lynott, with only Downey sticking it out with him as a member of the band until the bitter end in 1983.

BELOW: *A sight to gladden the hearts of all rock fans who were lucky enough to attend Thin Lizzy's spectacular concerts during the 1970s. The band's founder member and bassist Phil Lynott (centre) is flanked by guitarists Brian Robertson (left) and Scott Gorham (right).*

RIGHT: *Phil Lynott (right) with Gary Moore, in a typical mean and macho pose. Moore's temporary recruitment to Thin Lizzy as a guitarist in 1977 coincided with one of the most successful periods in the band's history.*

Bell had been a member of the early incarnation of Van Morrison's Them, while Downey came to Lizzy from a group called Sugar Shack, though he had also been a member of The Black Eagles. Wricksen soon departed the line-up.

Downey recently recalled the band's formative years: 'We had to play cover versions in the early days. Some of the places in the country wouldn't accept the band unless they included Top 20 material. I remember going down to a place in Carlow and the guy comes up to me and says there is no point in playing Jimi Hendrix or Queen music, you'd have to play something in the Top 10, and we just couldn't believe this mentality. We were used to playing anything we liked in Dublin.'

In 1971, Thin Lizzy released their eponymous debut album on the Decca label, and it topped the Radio Luxembourg charts for weeks on end, holding off **Ram,** Paul McCartney's second album as an ex-Beatle.

Making the breakthrough

Speaking at the time, Lynott, described by one British music journalist as 'tall, a beautiful shade of brown, Irish and thin', explained how much topping the Luxembourg 'Heavy Twenty' charts meant to them: 'Kid (Jensen, at that time a Radio Luxembourg DJ) liking the first album so much really made a difference. I mean, now say, if we go back home to Ireland we can fill up a hall with about two and a half thousand.'

In February 1973, the band's rocked up arrangement of the Irish traditional song 'Whiskey In The Jar' reached the Top 10 of the British charts. This was Lizzy's first taste of international success and, having undergone some severe personnel and management changes, they hit on their definitive line-up in 1974, when Downey and Lynott were joined by the ace guitarists Scott Gorham and Brian Robertson.

Gary Moore was to intermittently rejoin the group (he briefly preceded the Gorham/Robertson twin guitar incarnation), which was constantly stricken by ill health and other personal problems.

For many, the album **Jailbreak** (1976) still remains their finest hour, containing as it does the fist-waving, good-time macho

'I didn't get my first wooden guitar until I was nine, but I had a plastic one up until then, and I'd learned something from that. I went on stage for the first time a couple of weeks after I got that wooden guitar'

– RORY GALLAGHER.

strut of 'The Boys Are Back In Town', one of their greatest hits.

Tragically, Phil Lynott died in early 1986 as a consequence of his rock'n'roll lifestyle. His music combined melody with drive, and his subtlety and sensitivity in such a formidable macho-ridden genre has ensured that his legacy endures today.

In a 1971 *New Spotlight* magazine popularity poll, Pat Egan topped the Best Club DJ section, Skid Row were the top Non-Resident Irish Group, Thin Lizzy second and Rory Gallagher third. In the Irish-Based Group section, Horslips were number one, with Alyce second, and a tie for third place between Reform, Chips, Time Machine and Tomorrow's People. Slowly but surely, indigenous rock bands were loosening the grip of showband conservatism in Ireland.

Egan remembers going to a party in Phil Lynott's flat in Clontarf around about this time. 'It was the first dope party I was ever at. I was expecting drinks and food, but everybody was just lying around the floor listening to music. I was too straight, that was my problem!'

As 1972 drew to a close, bands and solo artists being tipped for success included Brogue (formerly Alyce), Brush (also known as Skid Row), Thin Lizzy, Van Morrison, Fruupp, Fudd (having dropped the Elmer adjunct), Tir Na nOg (the acoustic duo of Sonny Condell and Leo O'Kelly), Horslips and Rory Gallagher.

By then, Thin Lizzy had made two albums, Van Morrison had released *St Dominic's Preview*, his fifth for Warner Brothers, and Gallagher was voted World's Top Guitarist in Britain's *Melody Maker*. Tir Na nOg had moved to London in 1970, and by 1972 they had released two albums on Chrysalis – *Tir Na nOg* and *Tear And A Smile*. Irish acts were now creating something of an international stir.

However, that year the Irish rock scene was beset by a major set-back, with the news that Dublin's biggest rock venue, the National Stadium, would no longer be available for groups like Thin Lizzy and Rory Gallagher, who apparently caused a lot of 'raving' at their concerts.

Indeed rock's reputation as a subversive activity was further fuelled when, in September 1973, the new Skid Row started

ABOVE: *Horslips were able to present a visual image which was in keeping with an early 1970s rock band while having a major advantage over most of their rivals in that they could draw on their knowledge of Irish traditional music and folklore for inspiration.*

a mini-riot in Sligo in the west of Ireland, with fans causing £200 worth of damage to a local theatre. The venue promptly banned 'progressive' music and the incident was reported extensively in the national press.

The new Skid Row line-up featured Brush Shiels on bass, Ed Deane (formerly of Granny's Intentions) on lead guitar, ex-Taste drummer John Wilson and former Alyce singer Eamonn Gibney. After recording a new single – 'Dublin City Girls' – Wilson flew to London to fulfil prior commitments on a Led Zeppelin album.

A new direction

As the 1970s dawned, a new phenomenon called Celtic rock was bubbling under the collective rock psyche. This was instigated by Horslips, an unlikely collection of musicians, with art school, literary and advertising backgrounds. The definitive line-up included Eamon Carr (on drums), Jim Lockhart (keyboards/flute) Johnny Fean (guitar), Charles O'Connor (fiddle/mandolin), and Barry Devlin (bass). 'Johnny's Wedding' (1972) , their debut single, was a glorious fusion of rock and traditional influences, and it raced up the Irish charts.

Years later, Eamon Carr, now a rock journalist/broadcaster, recalled the band's

genesis. 'The origin of the Horslips crack was Tara Telephone, a poetry and music ensemble with Peter Fallon (brother of Bernard Patrick, a renowned chronicler of the rich and famous rock'n'roll élite) and Declan Sinnott (the first guitarist, now with folk singer Mary Black). To be perfectly honest with you, the Celtic rock thing was a complete accident.'

Carr and Charles O'Connor were asked to mime to a Harp lager commercial on Irish TV and began to hammer out a few songs together.

'We actually got together out of sheer boredom' Carr remembers, 'there was nothing to do. The beat scene was dead, with some of the bands into the guru Maharishi. It was really bad, horrible. Like you'd imagine the '40s or something.'

The nascent Celtic rock group were soon asked to audition for an Irish language music show on RTE television, and secured the part.

Eamon Carr: 'You can rehearse all you want, but once you do a gig, you're a band. We had a schizophrenic repertoire from the beginning. I was trying to get them to do John Lee Hooker songs, in among things like "The Mason's Apron" or Thunderclap Newman. We were just fucking around.'

With Irish music the brief for the show, the band spent an entire lunchtime in RTE agonising over a name. A rather inebriated friend who was with them suggested that they call themselves The Four Horsemen of the Apocalypse. Another joker laughingly suggested The Four Poxmen of the Horslypse. And that was that.

Horslips went professional on Saint Patrick's Day 1972, following the release of their single 'Johnny's Wedding'. Many aspiring Celtic rockers attempted to follow in the band's slipstream. However, Horslips remain the original and best, and even today they are fondly remembered by the likes of former Radiators From Space and current Pogues guitarist Phil Chevron, for bringing traditional-influenced rock music to a wider audience.

> '*When I said that I was a Black Irishman I was speaking objectively from an outsider's point of view, that people would figure it was a hard place to start from. But I always thought it made me special, unique. I knew I had something to offer and I had special determination to make it. In any case I think of myself as an Irishman first, black second*'
>
> – PHIL LYNOTT.

After several albums and a hectic touring schedule, Horslips had all but burned themselves out by the end of the decade. They had dabbled in everything from Celtic mysticism and concept albums like *The Tain* (1973) to American rock-influenced offerings like *The Man Who Built America* (1978). In 1980, they finally dissolved.

Musical missionaries

Horslips were to prove exceedingly influential in the overall development of Irish rock music, providing the impetus for countless other bands to get together. Their members had often been inspired by seeing Horslips live on stage. By playing in ballrooms throughout the country, they brought live rock music to an Irish audience who otherwise would have been reared on a particularly unappetising staple diet of showbands, country and the traditional Irish music.

The inclusion of traditional instruments in their line-up also paved the way for bands in the 1980s and 1990s, who used uilleann pipes and fiddles in a rock idiom. These included Moving Hearts, Stockton's Wing, In Tua Nua and Cry Before Dawn.

Ireland in the mid-1970s was a mixed-up musical maelstrom. Punk had yet to arrive and hippie music still hung over the land like a dark cloud. Along with a few second division progressive rock bands long past their sell-by date, country rock and pub rock was the standard fare.

Most of the established heroes like Van Morrison, Rory Gallagher, Horslips and Thin Lizzy had left the country for greener pastures. Larry Mullen of U2 had yet to pin

ABOVE: *The blank, decadent image which was presented to the world by The Boomtown Rats was endorsed by the antisocial lyrics of punk songs such as their 1977 British Top 20 hit 'Looking After No.1'.*

that note on the notice board in Mount Temple looking for musicians to form a band that would later conquer the world.

Many of the aforementioned successful acts were drawing on Irish mythology and romanticism or good old-fashioned musical credibility. Old dinosaurs meanwhile meandered about hopelessly adrift, tossing off interminable guitar solos while sporting flared trousers and lank locks. The first dawning of punk came as a welcome relief.

In 1976, the Falling Asunder Tour, featuring, among others, The Boomtown Rats and Nightbus (with Deke O'Brien, formerly of beat group Bluesville), attempted to inject some much-needed life into the ailing local Irish rock scene. In Britain, the Sex Pistols were singing of anarchy and the Queen, and getting up the non-safety pinned noses of those tax-exiled acts whose downfall they were ardently planning.

In Dublin's Moran's Hotel the sharp, knife-edged performances of visiting r'n'b acts like Eddie And The Hot Rods, were noted by The Rats, who played the same venue themselves on a regular basis. The Rats' hairstyles were soon shortened, drainpipe trousers replaced flapping flares, all facial hair was ruthlessly removed (Bob Geldof had once sported a fetching little moustache!) and a high velocity rhythm and blues repertoire was perfected.

Fronted by the gangly Geldof, who frankly admitted that his reasons for joining a band were to get famous, get rich and get laid, and not necessarily in that order, The Rats infused enormous energy and excitement into the scene. Attention focussed on Geldof, who stalked the stage looking like an amphetamine-fuelled reincarnation of a youthful Mick Jagger, complete with the lips, the swagger and the arrogance.

Other bands, like The Radiators From Space and The Vipers, wholeheartedly embraced the new music. At the time, moving to London was a necessary prerequisite to 'making it', and all three bands experienced varying degrees of success.

BELOW LEFT: *Bob Geldof belts out another song on stage with The Boomtown Rats. The inevitable comparisons between Geldof and Mick Jagger were inspired by their shared looks and energetic performances on stage. In 1985, Geldof managed to persuade his one-time idol to appear at the American Live Aid concert.*

ABOVE: *A youthful U2 at one with nature.*

'Our music is not punk, and it's not new wave' said Bob Geldof in Britain during 1977's summer explosion of punk. 'The Boomtown Rats are all about 1977 pop music, and if people don't like that, then screw 'em. We've brought the joy of rock'n'roll back to Ireland. We allowed other bands, The Vipers, The Radiators, The Gizmos to operate. We actually went out and created a rock circuit for them to work in. We were the first neighbourhood rock heroes to happen in ten years and we're proving the same over here, in the face of anything else that's happening.'

Classic punk

The Radiators' *Television Screen* (1977) was the work of angry young men intent on smashing the nearest TV tube with their Fender Telecasters instead of simply changing the channel. The band's second album, *Ghostown* (1979), is still regarded as an Irish classic, though it sold poorly at the time.

The punk/new wave gigs demanded that the audience participate. There was no sitting at the back of the room sipping a shandy in Moran's Hotel when The Radiators or The Rats played. Excitement, tension and the smell of sweat filled the air, and on stage guitar chords were slashed out at breakneck speed. A definite anti-authoritarian attitude prevailed.

By the late 1970s, the Dublin music scene was looking decidedly healthy, with bands such as The Blades, Revolver, DC Nien, U2, The Vultures, Chant Chant Chant, Rocky DeValera & The Gravediggers, The Atrix and The Virgin Prunes performing regularly. Besides Moran's Hotel in Talbot Street, Baggot Street's famed Baggot Inn, the Project Arts Centre in Essex Street and the Dandelion Market on Stephen's Green (now a plush shopping centre) were regular venues.

Of all the bands plying their wares at the time, U2 seemed least special. DC Nien were more exciting, The Blades had far better songs, The Vultures and Rocky DeValera's Gravediggers were more fun and The Virgin Prunes were occasionally gross but always entertaining.

In U2, The Edge had a neat guitar style, but their early numbers were more like well-planned musical exercises than inspirational songs. Bono, invariably clad in a black polo-neck jumper, was certainly an energetic frontman, who attempted with varying degrees of success to communicate with his then less-than-captive audience.

Initially called The Hype, the band had come together in 1976 at drummer Larry Mullen's instigation. Pushed and promoted at first by bassist Adam Clayton, who took on a managerial role of sorts, in April 1978

they won a competition sponsored by Harp lager and the *Evening Press* newspaper. The band soon attracted the attentions of future manager Paul McGuinness.

The well-spoken McGuinness, older than the band and with a background in film and video, was advised to check them out by local well-respected rock critic Bill Graham, with whom he had attended Trinity College. He liked what he saw, and a carefully orchestrated campaign resulted in the band signing to Island Records and taking on the world.

In September 1979, U2 released *U23* in Ireland on the CBS label. It was a three track EP featuring 'Out Of Control', 'Stories For Boys' and 'Boy/Girl'. Original copies now change hands for large amounts of money in U2 fanclub circles.

Instead of taking the emigrant trail the band opted to base themselves at home, using Dublin's Windmill Lane Studios for their early recordings. They didn't belong to any Irish tradition, and took their inspiration from the English post-punk scene as opposed to the USA, where blues, country and rock'n' roll had originated.

Following the release of their debut album, *Boy*, in 1980, they embarked on exhaustive tours of Europe and the USA. This was to be the norm for years to come, in between which some of the then highly religious members of the band wrestled with their consciences about the relationship between the devil's music and the Christian life. As the 1980s progressed, so too did U2's music, and by the time the album **The Unforgettable Fire** was released in 1984 (produced by Brian Eno and Daniel Lanois), there were definite rumblings afoot. Tracks like 'Pride' and 'Bad' hinted at a degree of greatness in the making.

Bono seemed born to play large venues and stadiums, frequently climbing atop speakers and scaffolding while the band's Big Music boomed out all around him. For many, a U2 performance became an almost religious celebration as Bono sought to inspire and stimulate his followers.

Messages in the music

He tackled weighty issues like spiritual renewal, prisoners of conscience and love and peace, while name-checking the dead American civil rights leader Martin Luther King. There were no rock star excesses and indulgences about U2. Instead, they supported Greenpeace, Anti-Apartheid and Amnesty International.

However, we would have to wait until **The Joshua Tree** (1987) for them to prove their true worth as songwriters. Content finally triumphed over style, and the combination of good songs with The Edge's highly individualistic guitar licks proved a winner. The band featured on the cover of the prestigious *Time* magazine, where they were labelled 'Rock's Hottest Ticket'.

Bono and the boys had finally arrived, and from then up until the present day their every itch and movement has been reported by a slavering local press corps. Bonowatch has proved to be a lucrative pastime for many rock journalists, documenting his every trip from home to studio to nightclub to maternity hospital to his brother's downtown Dublin restaurant.

Privacy remains of paramount importance, and in the late 1980s Bono coughed up £204,000 for a tiny one-room house which overlooked his property. Ironically, the story goes that Bono had casually informed some friends of his desire to buy it, and they all turned up to bid on his behalf, thereby drastically increasing the property's original £84,000 asking price.

> *'It went over the top, over the wall, very offside, ran across a few fields, did a real obstacle course and nearly drowned in a river. I think I know that I have to accept responsibility for the drowning. I mean, I single-handedly nearly pulled the band under with me, because I was drowning'*
>
> – BONO ON U2'S 'WAR' TOUR.

Meanwhile, debates raged about their pontificating, with some believing that the band were completely self-obsessed. Indeed, as they invested in more properties in Dublin and expanded their Mother record label, it looked as if they were systematically taking over the city.

An American odyssey

However, the band were nothing if not honest, admitting that they knew precious little about the roots of music. With that in mind, they were about to embark on a musical odyssey that would find them unreservedly embracing the land of the Big Mac. Already Bono's Red Indian appearance and The Edge's preacher man look had resulted in some criticism from certain quarters of the Irish press for their apparent undermining of Irish culture by this adoption of the trappings of the New World.

For the next album, **Rattle and Hum** (1988), they journeyed to Memphis to record in the famous Sun Studios, where Elvis Presley, Jerry Lee Lewis, Johnny Cash and Carl Perkins had once gathered around the piano for an informal sing-song. Had they come to pay homage or seek inspiration? Probably a combination of both.

They also 'adopted' legendary bluesman B.B. King, who was to regularly perform onstage with the band during their Lovetown tour. **Rattle and Hum** was a brave if ultimately foolhardy release, showing a vulnerable and naked U2, kneeling and learning at the feet of the real masters.

A different form of nakedness was to appear on **Achtung Baby** (1991), in the form of a full-frontal nude sleeve shot of bassist Adam Clayton. He reportedly insisted on its inclusion and manager Paul McGuinness 'joked' that Adam had threatened to quit the band if it wasn't used. At the 1992 Smithwicks/*Hot Press* Music Critics' Award ceremony Bono, while collecting the award for Best Album, humourously remarked that 'Adam Clayton has the smallest willy in U2'. This has yet to be documented.

Back in harness with the production team of Lanois and Eno, the album found

the band exploring new territory, with tales of disharmony and love gone wrong. The musical influences were of a more European nature, sections of the album having been recorded in Berlin's celebrated Hansa Studio, as used by *Low/Lodger/Heroes* period David Bowie and reformed rock wildman Iggy Pop.

The ghosts of the band's American dream/nightmare had been exorcised and U2 proved that they still had something left to say. *Achtung Baby* demanded full attention, as it took the listener on an emotional roller coaster ride.

While U2 came to international prominence in the 1980s, back home in Ireland they left a trail of destruction and broken dreams in their wake. Hundreds of bands attempted to emulate the U2 'sound', as British and American record companies descended on Dublin, all waving cheque books and raving about the 'next U2'.

A host of Irish artists were signed to international deals, most notably In Tua Nua, Aslan, Cactus World News, The Fountainhead, Les Enfants, Blue In Heaven, Light A Big Fire, Tuesday Blue and Cry Before Dawn. They were all unceremoniously dropped when their talent failed to translate itself into record sales. The harsh economic realities of the music business soon came home to scores of Irish musicians who overnight were consigned to the scrap heap.

All were unable to crack either the American or the British markets, having been swept along by a huge wave of optimism and precious little else. Aslan, In Tua Nua, Cactus World News and Blue In Heaven in particular had burned brightly but only briefly.

Beset by business problems the well-respected Blades finally broke up in 1986, with Paul Cleary forming a new, but short-

RIGHT: *After a three year hiatus, U2 returned to the top of the charts in 1991 with the album* Achtung Baby. *The band's moody and mysterious look on the album sleeve was matched by the new recorded material.*

lived band called The Partisans with guitar hotshot Conor Brady. They were to remain as something of a well-kept secret from the record company talent scouts. Most of the contenders from the class of the mid-1980s had dispersed, with their hopes of fame and all of its trappings having endured the painful Burning Spitfire Syndrome. Only the outspoken Sinead O'Connor (the Dublin-born singer/songwriter who had her

> *'I remember playing the Baggot Inn with U2. They used to disgust us. But they were just kids then, middle class kids... though Bono says he's from Ballymun. I think that when they were starting, it was a help to them; to be afraid, to not be sort of shy, as working class kids can be. Middle class kids don't mind expressing themselves. They're encouraged to do that. That helps'*
>
> – PAUL CLEARY OF THE BLADES.

biggest hit with her interpretation of the Prince song 'Nothing Compares 2 U') and, to a certain extent, Hothouse Flowers, were to come close to emulating U2's massive international success. Apart from that, it was back to the rehearsal room and the pub to dream of what might have been. Or, worse still, the dole queue and the realisation of a misspent 10 years. At the turn of the decade a new generation of bands were signed to various labels. An Emotional Fish, Power Of Dreams, A House, The Black Velvet Band, The Fat Lady Sings, The Forget Me Nots, Blink, The Pale, Housebroken and Andrew Strong all have international record deals. How they fare remains to be seen.

Despite the 99 per cent failure rate in the music business, U2 have managed to make playing rock'n'roll a respectable occupation. Even incidents such as Adam Clayton's 1989 brush with the law over cannabis possession, couldn't deter mothers and fathers throughout the land from encouraging their musically-inclined offspring to join a band and see the world.

In retrospect, most of them would have done just as well by joining their country's navy. It should be noted that the Irish navy does not in fact go anywhere.

> *'I did find it quite ironic that The Undertones couldn't even give away records. Maybe the people who liked The Undertones never really had enough money to buy our records. It might have just been a case of pure and hard economics – the starving student brigade!'*
>
> – FEARGAL SHARKEY.

I T'S GENERALLY RECOGNISED THAT, AS a breeding ground for young talent within a rock'n'roll milieu, Northern Ireland hasn't been found wanting. Since the mid-1960s, the six counties of the North have spawned a wide variety of rock bands and artists who have enjoyed international commercial appeal while retaining musical integrity; an unusual combination.

In the late 1950s and early 1960s, Belfast sang and danced to the sounds of showbands. These bastions of unoriginality and musical conservatism effectively ruled the entertainment arenas both North and South of the border. However, one of them – The Monarchs – were unusual in that their instrumentation led itself to include the upfront use of harmonicas and guitars rather than the ubiquitous brass section. Another curious aspect of The Monarchs was their cover versions: instead of rifling the late 1950s British charts for suitably gross post-Elvis Presley suppertime cabaret songs, the band copied the songs of American rock'n'roll chart hits.

A member of The Monarchs from 1959, 14-year-old George Ivan Morrison wanted to bring his own influences into the group.

LEFT: *Van Morrison, the major figure in Irish rock music since the 1960s, and still going strong in the 1990s.*

His family background of country, gospel and blues, and the recent upsurge of American rhythm'n'blues – infamously internationalised by a pelvis-wiggling Elvis Presley – had a lasting impression on Morrison and The Monarchs, but their too-rough sound was out of time if not place.

Wandering minstrels

The Monarchs left Belfast for Glasgow and thence to London, where they were put in touch with the American Armed Forces PX club circuit in Germany. There, Morrison played with Armed Forces negro musicians, dynamically improvising treatments of James Brown, John Lee Hooker and Ray Charles songs. Following a harrowing schedule, The Monarchs returned to Belfast and promptly split up, with Morrison venturing to London yet again in his search for like-minded musicians to form a *real* r'n'b band, playing *original* material.

After several fruitless weeks, Van returned to his native city, empty-handed and broke. By the close of the year, though, his luck turned around – he discovered amongst one of the many Belfast showbands, The Gamblers, a guitarist named Bill Harrison. By the beginning of 1964, Them was a reality, and it is with Them that the story of Belfast as a recognizable and valid – indeed, often underrated – centre of rock'n'roll begins.

The original members of Them in 1964 were: Van Morrison (vocals, harmonica), Alan Henderson (bass), Bill Harrison (guitar), Ronnie Millings (drums) and Eric Wricksen (piano). Obtaining a residency in Belfast's Maritime Hotel, Them's urgency and energy was soon picked up on by appreciative teenagers. The band signed to the Decca record label – home also to The Rolling Stones – and left Belfast in mid-1964 for London to record material that

RIGHT: *One man and his guitar against the world. Van Morrison takes on the fashionable hippie look. Unlike many of his late 1960s/early 1970s contemporaries, he has drawn on his own country's Celtic mysticism rather than looking to eastern cultures for inspiration.*

would later surface as their debut hit single (strangely enough, a cover version, despite Morrison's own feelings on self-composed material) 'Baby, Please Don't Go'. On the B-side was 'Gloria', largely ignored at the time, but later to become the band's most enduring number.

There was, inevitably – and quite naturally – a distinct feeling of optimism among the rock'n'roll denizens of Belfast. Here, for the first time, was a golden opportunity for local lads to take on the world, if not initially on their own terms then certainly at a later date. One of the original bunch of Belfast youths who actually waved goodbye to Them from Belfast dock jetty was the perennially enthusiastic Terry Hooley, an integral figure in the development of Northern Irish music. He remembers the atmosphere in Belfast thus: 'There was a definite sense of hope about Them, but what you've got to take into consideration was that not everybody had the same breaks as Morrison's band. Aside from Them, there were a lot of really good bands around at the time – people like Sam Mahoud And The Big Soul Band. Sam was the James Brown of Belfast; he used to break down and cry on stage! Fantastic...

'Other great bands operating in the same area as Them – that rough-house r'n'b/soul vein – were The Alley Katz, The Just Five and The Aztecs. Rhythm and blues was quite a strong thing in Belfast, with clubs like Sammy Houston's and the Maritime Hotel's being just two of around 80 r'n'b-type venues. This meant that some bands would go and play three gigs on a Friday or Saturday night.'

Chart success
With 'Baby, Please Don't Go' crashing into the British Top 10 and seriously denting the American charts, it looked as if the world was indeed theirs for the taking. The follow-up single, 'Here Comes The Night', reached the Top 3 in Britain in the spring of 1965, but all was not well in the band. Management and personnel difficulties prevailed from mid-1965 to the following year, during which Them recorded two albums – **Angry Young Them** and **Them Again** – the end product of which thoroughly upset Morrison. Following an American tour with The Doors and Love, Them reached the point of no return, leaving Morrison back in Belfast with a sour taste

in his mouth regarding both his involvement with the music industry and with a permanent band set-up. He left soon after, but Them carried on a patchy post-Morrison career of their own until 1971, the group even reforming for a German tour in the late 1970s before finally calling it a day.

In retrospect, Them, although an unrefined product of their times and the originators of some tautly wrought r'n'b, will be remembered for their first couple of singles and as the band that spurred Van Morrison on to a solo career. That career has helped place Belfast and Northern Ireland on the international music map and has given it a sense of time and place. Interestingly, however, Morrison has never commented on the political situation in that part of Ireland.

Van Morrison's recording career and life has engendered reams of hagiographical reportage and comment. He's seen as one of the all-time greats in rock music *per se*, and not just in Irish terms. His poetic and lyrical vision has transcended both time and barriers, while being almost simultaneously inspiring and embarrassing.

The roots of his muse are the often perplexing combinations of literary sensibility, nirvana-like stream-of-consciousness states

> '*Everybody asks the same first question, the same second question... Is it okay if I go to sleep?*'
>
> – *VAN MORRISON.*

LEFT: *After serving his apprenticeship with various Irish bands during the late 1960s and early 1970s, Gary Moore went on to spend time with Thin Lizzy before enjoying success as a solo artist in the hard rock and blues mould.*

of mind, and a winning way with a memorable melody. This creative mixture was never more evident than on his third solo album, *Astral Weeks* (1968). His first two albums, *Blowin' Your Mind* and *The Best Of Van Morrison* (both 1967), had both been fairly ordinary (especially in comparison to his later work), save the epic, distressing 10 minutes of the former's 'T. B. Sheets', which heralded Van's future preoccupation with non-pop tunes.

Astral Weeks was recorded in a mere two days and showcased Van's increasingly able vocal stylising – formatively utilised on some of Them's recordings – and his creative use of the pop lyric as poetry. This seminal album has been accorded classic status by both pundits and fans alike, and, like all enduring works of music, continues to sell, although it wasn't a major commercial success at the time of its release, not even charting in Britain.

Van's follow-up, *Moondance*, (1970) utilised a tighter control on the manner in which he structured the songs and there was less room for improvisational, ambient space. More compact and therefore more readily accessible, *Moondance* was a commercial success – it was his first album to enter the British charts, peaking at just outside the Top 30 – as well as a critical one.

Still living and recording in the USA, Morrison and his entourage moved to Woodstock, a move indicative of the spirit of the times and one that transferred its associated mien of looseness and relaxation to his music. Both *Van Morrison: His Band And The Street Choir* (1970) and *Tupelo Honey* (1971) are products of this pungent era. The former is one of Morrison's worst albums, lacking form, strategy and lucidity; the latter reflects his fondness for rustic Americana, and was almost a country album. Morrison wasn't thoroughly satisfied with this album – a professional trait that shadows him to the present day – but it sold well enough.

If *Tupelo Honey* generates enough downhome emotional well-being, his next album, *St Dominic's Preview* (1972) describes his love-lost state of mind over his marriage difficulties. One of Morrison's occasionally exceptional albums, the songs on *Preview* are acoustic-based, and reveal a man and his guitar wailing against the ills of his personal world. The title track also contains the first memorable reference to his native city and to one of his many labouring jobs – cleaning windows (this episode in his life was to be mentioned again on Morrison's *Beautiful Vision* album 10 years later).

Diversification and growth

For the next 10 years – from 1973 to 1983 – Van Morrison was to release albums of various musical styles. They also varied in terms of their quality, strength and beauty. Throughout each – *Hard Nose The Highway* (1973), *It's Too Late To Stop Now* (1974), *Veedon Fleece* (1974), *A Period Of Transition* (1977), *Wavelength* (1978), *Into The Music* (1979), *Common One* (1980), *Beautiful Vision* (1982) and *Inarticulate Speech Of The Heart* (1983) – his personal aesthetic of a deeply spiritual and questioning nature comes to the fore.

> '*I understand Van Morrison... He enjoys the privacy of not having to give his telephone number... My understanding is that he's maybe like all of us... Just as lonely as the rest of us*'
>
> – JOHN T. DAVIS, FILM MAKER.

Some of these albums have attained the status of 'Great Van Morrison Albums', in particular the live double album *It's Too Late...* and *Common One*. The remainder are reminders of Morrison's contribution to a body of work that takes in constituents of a distinctly religious and elemental nature. They're also a body of work that continuously, albeit through enigmatic or abstruse lyrical structures, refer to Morrison's past and present feelings about his birthplace.

Even his studio albums from 1983 onwards – *A Sense Of Wonder* (1985), *No Guru, No Method, No Teacher* (1986), *Poetic Champions Compose* (1987), *Irish Heartbeat* (with The Chieftains, 1988), *Avalon Sunset* (1989), *Enlightenment* (1990) and *Hymns To The Silence* (1991) – have a definite sense of time and place about them, as if Morrison was becoming increasingly intent on delving further into a quasi-spiritual confusion and coming up with some ambiguous answers to complex questions.

A genuine star

Despite his many detractors, Morrison has contributed greatly to both rock music and to a general understanding of rock music as a means of artistic expression and vision. He could well be the most unlikely-looking rock star since Bill Haley (the unconvincing and sanitised version of commercial rock'n'roll), but there's no denying his gifts of communication and creativity.

In the context of Northern Ireland, however, Morrison seems to be curiously detached from the prevailing situation. While a large amount of his work wrestles with his very personal concepts of Celtic mysticism – executed within any and every musical framework – pop, jazz, blues, traditional, country, classical, spoken word – troublesome aspects regarding his place of origin rarely, if ever, feature in his work. He visits Belfast more often now, perhaps laying aside old ghosts and memories.

He does appear to be able to release albums with sometimes alarming frequency. Morrison's profligacy could well turn to his disadvantage, especially if he continues making music of such similar variety. The 'Belfast Cowboy', however, should run and run, for what he does he does exceptionally well. He has no competitors.

Throughout Van Morrison's lengthy career he spent a lot of time outside Northern Ireland carving an international name for himself and ensuring that he would retain lifelong credibility in the public eye. But what of home? When Morrison left Belfast in the late 1960s, it could be argued that he left a void in his birthplace that hasn't yet been filled in either musical or commercial terms. After the success of the indigenous Northern Irish beat boom groups of the mid-1960s, such as Ballymena's The Gentry and Portadown's The People (soon to mutate into Eire Apparent), little happened in the Six Counties of the North between the late 1960s and the mid-1970s.

The only major Northern Irish names to make their breakthrough during this period were the guitarists Rory Gallagher and Gary Moore and the progressive band Fruupp. Gallagher is reputed to have 'invaded' Belfast from his home turf of Cork in the late 1960s. With his band Taste, he virtually set up house and home in The Maritime Hotel and various r'n'b clubs dotted around the city.

Unlike Gallagher, Gary Moore was a native of Belfast, who left the city soon after his 16th birthday for Dublin and guitar roles with Skid Row, Granny's Intentions, Dr. Strangely Strange and Thin Lizzy. Moore is a maverick, restive personality who has built up a quite considerable reputation for himself as being both hard working and hard playing. His fluid but forceful guitar-playing technique has encompassed varying styles over the years. He has wrestled with melodic rock in Thin Lizzy, jazz/rock fusion in Colosseum II, and tight, hard rock in G-Force.

He is currently working in the blues mould – his first love and influence – and it would be fair to say that Moore has made no lasting contribution to the development of Northern Ireland as a recognizable musical entity. He has instead developed an assured musical persona and international guitar hero status.

Curiously, even though he spends most of his time outside of his home country, Moore is still lauded as being an 'Irish guitarist' rather than as a guitar player who just happens to have been born in Ireland. The sole exception to this apparent distancing of himself from his native land is *Wild Frontier* (1987), a fine Celtic rock album of some authority and legitimacy.

ABOVE: *Up-and-coming singer/song-writer Andy White plays a set outside Belfast's Good Vibrations record shop, the nerve centre of all that is good in Northern Irish rock music.*

BELOW RIGHT: *Rudi, the punk band whose dynamic concerts in the late 1970s helped convince Belfast music guru Terry Hooley that music had come alive once again in his city.*

As for the Belfast group, Fruupp, these early 1970s techno-rockers are but a minor footnote: their four albums for the Dawn record label all flopped. In contrast, Belfast-based singer David McWilliams made his name in 1967 with his debut single 'The Days Of Pearly Spencer' and followed it with three British Top 40 albums.

Fast forward to the mid-1970s and punk rock and Belfast's Good Vibrations record label. Fasten your safety belts – you're in for a bumpy ride!

'It was the punks who brought the nightlife back into Belfast, going to gigs in The Harp and The Pound venues.' So says Northern Irish rock savant and saviour Terry Hooley, founder of Good Vibrations. If it hadn't been for Hooley and his catalystic record label there wouldn't have been a Northern Irish 'scene' at that time.

'People didn't go into the city centre at night. The only people you'd see there would be a few winos and lots of punks going to The Harp bar. It really was like that. People like Jim Armstrong from Them was still playing in some venues, so that r'n'b thing was still going on, although on a low profile. It wasn't as if anything was

really happening – just a few older musicians playing for the enjoyment of it, ageing hippies like myself. But the punk thing was the first time in over 10 years that all the kids came from all the ghettos and it didn't matter whether you were a Protestant or a Catholic as long as you were a punk. Without a doubt. Even the punk thing in Belfast got a lot of people who were around from the 1960s going to gigs again to see the new bands.'

Hooley remembers the thrill of seeing young teenage bands playing music that he, as a teenager, had loved: 'It was quite exciting for someone like me, who'd been into American garage bands such as The Seeds, The Standells, ? And The Mysterions, all these bands you'd find on various *Nuggets* compilation albums.

'A lot of the punk bands were influenced by these sounds. The first time I went to a gig, Rudi were playing The Who's 'My Generation', ? And The Mysterions '96 Tears' – I got so excited by this! It was my youth coming back, because I hadn't been going out much to gigs what with the Troubles, and I creamed my jeans over this. On that first night, the police came in and

all the kids started shouting "SS RUC". Then the next thing that happened was the UDR (Ulster Defence Regiment) came in and the kids started throwing things at them. I thought, "This is for me. This is fucking brilliant. This is what I've been waiting for all my life.'"

Another person who was just waiting for something to happen was the then burgeoning film maker, John T. Davis. Davis was so excited by bands such as The Outcasts and Protex, and by the whole movement, that he made film documentaries about them. The most famous is *Shellshock Rock*,

a warts and all look at the new and growing Northern Ireland punk rock scene. With hand-held camera and dodgy shooting angles, *Shellshock Rock* captures both time and place with both urgency and deliberation. Davis remembers those early days: 'It was a very special couple of creative years that was happening... I know it's sort of died a death, but back in the late 1970s it was wonderful, a real positive step forward for kids – the rejection of traditional values, and the unification of Catholic and Protestant, rock'n'roll, punk, whatever, brought them together and at the time I

ABOVE: *Looking anything but the sophisticated performer he was later to become, singer Feargal Sharkey (second from right) poses with The Undertones at the beginning of their pop/punk career.*

to happen. Probably more bands formed in the Good Vibrations shop than anywhere else. The last thing it was was a proper shop and record label.'

Hooley accepts that if Good Vibrations hadn't been there to crystalise the formative fumblings of a dispossessed, hugely talented and starry-eyed youth then the scene wouldn't have been as influential or lasted as long. 'We had a fairly good suss. But we weren't interested in making money. That was like going against everything we believed in; that's why we never had contracts with the bands or anything like that. Once Good Vibrations started getting going, all the people who had made their money from various things tried to form their own punk labels. They used to have these meetings – so I was informed later on! – discussing why Good Vibrations' records kept selling like hot cakes. They felt it was something like the record covers, but the simple reason was that they didn't have a clue what was going on in the street, which is basically where we were.

Peel appeal

'We hated record companies. I just wanted to let people know that there was something happening here. At that time, almost every record company had forgotten about Northern Ireland. It was like that when I went to London – every record company threw me out with The Undertones' "Teenage Kicks". Rough Trade told me it was the worst record they'd ever heard. I arrived back in Belfast on a Monday night, broke down and cried. Before I left London, however I dropped off a copy of the single to John Peel, so that night I listened to his radio programme. He stuck it on, played it, said it was the most wonderful record he'd ever heard in his life and then played it twice in a row.

'Seymour Stein of Sire records phoned me next morning and The Undertones were signed up two days later. On the Friday, after John Peel had been playing the single every night, CBS – who physically threw me out of their offices – and all these other bastards started phoning! Everybody in the world wanted a copy of the record then.'

Thanks to Hooley's persistence and Peel's enthusiasm, The Undertones opened the floodgates for other Northern Irish punk rock groups to play, record and release singles equally as thrilling and pertinent to their emotional and social lives.

The Undertones formed in Derry in 1974, five teenagers with terrible dress sense

thought it was worthwhile filming it. It inspired me and gave me hope.'

Every movement needs a starting point and a figurehead. If it could be argued that Terry Hooley was not so much a figurehead as a benign autocrat in relation to Northern Irish punk, then without doubt his record shop and subsequent record label, Good Vibrations, was that movement's pioneering spirit. Hooley maintains that, almost throughout its initial history, Good Vibrations was a joke. 'It wasn't run like a record company – it was run more like a community, a shop where kids met every Saturday. There were so many kids the customers couldn't get in to buy anything. Ridiculous. It was a nerve centre for things

LEFT: *In his stage performances with The Undertones, Feargal Sharkey managed to combine raw sexuality with a 'little boy lost' look.*

and a great knack for playing cute renditions of old r'n'b songs and other assorted pop standards. The line-up was Damian O'Neill (lead guitar), Mickey Bradley (bass), Billy Doherty (drums), John O'Neill (rhythm guitar) and Feargal Sharkey (vocals). Initially, it was Sharkey's high-pitched, serene, choirboy voice that got the group noticed, but after a while the lyrics and tunes provided by John and Damian O'Neill came to the fore.

Following 'Teenage Kicks' with a succession of hit singles and appearances on *Top Of The Pops*, The Undertones decided to give up their day jobs and go completely professional. Their debut and follow up albums, *The Undertones* (1979) and *Hypnotised* (1980), were nigh on perfect examples of the persuasive powers of a skilful integration of pop's sweetness and punk's aggression.

Subsequent albums, *Positive Touch* (1981) and *The Sin Of Pride* (1983), evinced a disaffection with teenage traits as the group delved into the 1960s for musical inspiration and their maturing selves for lyrical motivation.

The end of the road

Creatively, the group was on to a winning formula, but commercially their star began to wane. Inevitable financial and musical differences cropped up and The Undertones split up in the summer of 1983, but not before they gave a fitting valedictory gig at an open air festival in aid of *Hot Press* at Punchestown Racecourse. 'I never understood it then and I don't understand it now,' says Feargal Sharkey on the disparity between The Undertones' critical and commercial evaluation.

It's different nowadays. Since the split, Sharkey has gone on to enjoy a significant amount of solo success, while some of his erstwhile colleagues have had minor status appeal with That Petrol Emotion. With The Undertones, Sharkey didn't write any of the lyrics (in many ways, Sharkey is the ultimate supreme voice in constant search for good songs). Songwriting was largely John O'Neill's duty, and when The Undertones parted he set up a band with his Undertone brother Damian, Raymond Gorman (guitar) and Ciaran McLaughlin (drums).

The foursome soon found themselves in London, discovering in American Steve Mack a suitable vocalist. Setting themselves up as far more of a socially and politically relevant pop group than The Undertones could ever be, That Petrol Emotion released their debut album, *Manic Pop Thrill* (1986) to tumultuous appraisal. Like the few singles preceding it, the album's inner sleeve was adorned with anti-British notes, even containing a passage from Irish Republican Michael Davitt's 1904 tract, *The Fall Of Feudalism In Ireland*. There was no doubt as to where That Petrol Emotion were coming from – definitely political and very definitely angry. Needless to say, their superbly structured agit-pop – the zenith of which is the single 'Big Decision' (1986) – made for great listening outside the mainstream charts. The follow-up, 'Babble' (1987), was even more successful. Staying in the Top 30 for three weeks, That Petrol Emotion had arrived, their combination of jagged-edged pop and take-it-or-leave-it lyrical bite strik-

> *'I was like Joe Public telling the guys in the band that this is the way he's going to react. They wanted to put the IRA in some kind of socio-economic context... But I felt putting those three letters in would immediately prejudice people'*
>
> – STEVE MACK, LEAD SINGER, THAT PETROL EMOTION.

RIGHT: *That Petrol Emotion; dazzling songs of protest and fire from the band that rose phoenix-like from the remnants of The Undertones.*

LEFT: *Steve Mack, the American singer with That Petrol Emotion, struts his stuff on stage.*

ing a chord with more than just the critics. Their third album, ***End Of Millennium Psychosis Blues*** (1988), was poorly received but this was counterbalanced two years later by ***Chemicrazy***, a return to form in terms of songwriting – they've largely dispensed with their political agenda – and song design. That Petrol Emotion were the only band who were singing and writing with some credibility about the political situation in Northern Ireland during the late 1980s. Ten years previously, that noble task

lay at the able feet – which were soon after to turn to clay – of Stiff Little Fingers. Of all the bands to emerge from the Northern Irish punk movement, they were the most controversial and the most exciting.

Following a spell with hard rockers Highway Star, the band was formed by Jake Burns (vocals/guitar), with Henry Cluney (rhythm guitar), Brian Faloon (drums), and Ali McMordie (bass). Stiff Little Fingers were the aural simulation of their city's social and political rupturings.

ABOVE: *Stiff Little Fingers produced powerful music by channelling their anger and frustration at the political situation in Northern Ireland into their songs.*

During their brief starburst of a career, the band had as many followers as detractors. Claims of chicanery were levelled at the band, following their management deal and co-songwriting activities with English journalist Gordon Ogilvie.

Ogilvie, over in Belfast to cover the 'Troubles' for an English tabloid, fell in with the band after seeing them play a gig of unusual ferocity. Duly impressed – and, no doubt, his journalistic instincts aroused by the odour of a good story – he and Jake Burns started to write several songs together. The results were – and still are – astonishing, unleashing two of the most crucial punk rock songs ever written. Both the debut single, 'Suspect Device', and its follow-up, 'Alternative Ulster', (both 1978) encapsulated everything that the disaffected youth felt about the situation in the North. It didn't matter what religion the listener was: here were two songs that transcended narrow boundaries and got right to the heart of the matter.

Politics aside – a difficult subject to avoid when discussing early Stiff Little Fingers – the songs themselves were classic, scratchy punk rants of the period. Agit-pop never sounded as essential or as angry. The band, of course, had their vehement critics, especially when publicity stunts – such as wrapping up review copies of their debut single in 'suspect device'-type packages, and the reproduction of explosives and British Army marksman photographs for the two singles covers – were utilised.

> *'Suspect Device was life to us. Besides, as soon as we moved to London we never wrote another song about the North'*
>
> – HENRY CLUNEY, GUITARIST, STIFF LITTLE FINGERS.

Too hot to handle

Ultimately, though, Stiff Little Fingers' early music saved them from media slaughter, although not many record companies were eager to place the band on their rosters. The combination of Stiff Little Fingers' political stance and growing reputation for tangibly violent, hair-raising concerts was beginning to take its toll on their commercial chances. When their fiery debut album, *Inflammable Material* (1979), was independently released, however, some of the majors watched with more than interest when it broke into the Top 20, and stayed in the charts for almost 20 weeks.

Eventually signed by Chrysalis, Stiff Little Fingers released a further five albums (including a live and a compilation set) for the label before they split up. By the end of their career, they had managed to stick close to their original intentions regardless of whether their critics liked it or not. But as for finally calling it a day... well, old punks never die, they just reform and adapt. Over the years, Stiff Little Fingers

have regrouped several times, initially to play some St. Patrick's Day concerts.

In 1991, they officially reformed, with Burns and Cluney being the only original members – drums were played by Dolphin Taylor, who had previously been a band member following the departure of Jim Reilly (who in turn replaced original drummer, Brian Faloon), while the bass guitar duties were given to Bruce Foxton, one time stalwart of British punk/mod band The Jam. *Flags And Emblems*, their late 1991 album release, was a collection of songs so far removed from the essence of the band as to do them and their fans a disservice. Not a very good way to remember a band who, during their glory-glory heydays, were as vital and as pertinent as anything that could be found in rock music. For those moments alone, Stiff Little Fingers will be justifiably remembered and celebrated.

Supporting players

There were many other lesser known, yet still indispensable – and cherished – Northern Irish groups who came and went in the blink of an eye. The list is as long as it is impressive: Rudi, The Starjets, Protex, The Outcasts, Big Self, The Tearjerkers, The Bankrobbers, The Male Caucasians, Crisis, Ruefrex, The X Dreamysts, Katmandu, The Moondogs, Shock Treatment... They all conspired to communicate various messages – teenage angst and frustration, Northern Irish tragedy and exultation, and weird thoughts on everyone and everything – in a form of music that outwardly seemed as frivolous and trivial as good pop music, but inwardly was as profound a form of expression as great rock music. This was aural literature, and the essence of what lasting rock'n'roll could and should be. If anything, the music emanating from Northern Ireland during this period (essentially between 1978 and 1980) more appropriately encapsulated the time and the place than its Southern counterpart. This point could be argued over, but what couldn't be is the wonderfully loud, fractious, utterly inspiring music.

Ten years on, the scene has ineradicably changed. Where can it go from here? Certainly, Terry Hooley isn't exactly full of optimism. 'I know more about the music

> '*Rock'n'roll cuts through all the shit and can appeal to an auld fella of 65 or a wee lad of five or six, once it's pure and true... it doesn't even have to be articulate*'
>
> – BRENDAN MURPHY, SINGER, THE 4 OF US.

RIGHT: *The 4 Of Us:
a Northern Irish
band who have the
potential for inter-
national success in
the 1990s.*
BELOW RIGHT: *Andy
White has shaken
off the initial com-
parisons that pre-
sented him as the
Northern Irish Bob
Dylan to establish
himself as an
accomplished
singer/songwriter in
his own right.*

business now and I still hate it,' he laughs. 'I'm still basically a fan, so I just let the bands get on with it. I still love going to see bands and I get really inspired sometimes by bands such as The Mighty Fall and Four Idle Hands, but the economic climate isn't exactly thriving...'

There are other hopes, of course, most notably The 4 Of Us. Others are Tiberious Minnows, The Carrelines (featuring ex-Undertones drummer Billy Doherty), Ashanti, Ghost Of An American Airman, The Divine Comedy, The Mighty Fall and many more. In a different field altogether is Belfast troubadour Andy White. He has a reputation as a singer/songwriter with a finger on the pulse of what's happening socially and politically. He also has a zealous following, but it's debatable whether he has the will to extend his presently folk-structured domain. He does have the combination of ready wit and an enduring appeal that might turn things in his favour.

The final comment on the present state of the Northern Irish muse must, unfortunately, be one of disappointment and disillusion, of hopes dashed, optimism grounded. 'When the Troubles came,' relates Terry Hooley, (whose Good Vibrations shop was damaged in a bomb blast in March 1992) 'there occurred a bigger displacement of population in Belfast than in any other city in Europe since World War II. A lot of the

> *'We write modern Belfast
> songs for everyone, but
> our perspective is straight
> down the middle. We're
> not putting up barriers'*
>
> *– ANDY WHITE.*

people who played in bands were the first to get out, because they were used to travelling. For example, way back when there used to be 40 of us – we were known as "The Tribe". We were all hippies. I ran a blues club and we were doing these underground magazines. Now, I'm the only one left in Belfast; everyone else is in Paris or Melbourne or New York or London...

'We lost a lot of good people when the Troubles came along. They all just left; people that I call the poets, painters and performers of the blues. A lot of richness and a lot of talent was lost. I sometimes wonder what would have happened if some of those people had stayed.'

OCK

> *'We're an Irish rock'n'roll band, and our ambition is to bring the lounge bar atmosphere of the West of Ireland to the world stage.'*
>
> – DAVY CARTON, LEAD SINGER, THE SAW DOCTORS.

IT'S ONLY IN THE PAST 10 YEARS OR SO that non-Irish ears have become accustomed to hearing Irish ethnic music on an international, commercial scale. Prior to this, Irish traditional music was looked upon as either a musical backwater or an impenetrable mess of rhythms and airs best left alone to the experts. Now, the general area of traditional music is opening up and diversifying, although the purists would say that such experimentation is causing its disintegration.

The definition of the word 'traditional' depends on a number of things, the most important of which is whether or not you believe that a tradition is something that is passed on through the years. To many people – Irish or otherwise – traditional music can mean The Clancy Brothers or De Danann, Christy Moore or The Saw Doctors. All of these are equally acceptable if somewhat ill-defined. In reality, what defines a tradition – extant or extinct – is whether or not the music and lyrics have been passed on by word of mouth. This oral transmission of music and words is principal to an understanding of what traditional music is and how it has survived. In Ireland, oral transmission of the music makes the country unique in that – unlike some countries in Europe, where traditional music has been almost parodied over the years – the playing hasn't changed.

What we hear today is essentially the ordinary Irish dance music of the 18th and 19th centuries and we are able to hear it by

LEFT: *Clannad drew strongly on their heritage to create their distinctive Irish music.*

virtue of its own method of transmission, which took place following the Irish famine of the mid-19th century. When Irish people took the boats to the USA at this time all they brought from their culture was dance music and a tradition of storytelling. They could only carry what was socially, culturally, or intellectually crucial to them, what their environment gave them: speech and music. These two things were brought to the American East Coast by the Irish, a people who then constructed both buildings and the country's internal network of railroads. As the people dispersed, the songs and music were distributed.

Travelling musicians

'The traditional music that is in Ireland today,' says Philip King, member of Scullion, musicologist and originator of the television documentary on Irish traditional music, *Bringing It All Back Home,* 'is integrally formed by its American experience, because the way in which it survived was that it travelled. It remained in many parts of the States in its pure form as well, but we get into a complex sociological order here because when the Irish arrived they were the poorest and the lowest of the low. But they were white, which meant that after a while they could assimilate and develop a different accent – they could be seen to be part of the American dream.

'They began to assume political power and the more they went up the social ladder the more they came to a dilemma. Which was, yes, they had a hankering for where they came from; yes, they had a belief that what they represented as Irish people was good, but still they wanted to deny the heavy duty racist aspect of the way in which they lived and what they had to do to survive. They are the people for whom the song "I'll Take You Home Again, Kathleen" became the true nature of Irish music, and they also began to forget other things like dance music.'

In the meantime, the traditional music being played on the East Coast had to adapt to the environment of New York and its hinterlands – in other words it had to be played faster for it to survive in bustling, urban areas. But the most strategic advance in the development of traditional Irish music was that its transmission changed from oral to disc. For the first time, it could be transported without recourse to the oral transmission convention. Such records were sent back home to Ireland, which is where the real story begins.

Philip King: 'When the music came back from the States to small places all around the 32 counties of Ireland, everybody wanted to copy the style that came from America. In effect, a pan-Irish style of playing developed whereby the local style of playing began to die out. But now that music is becoming true to its own region. So the music is truly traditional in that sense – an interpersonal, orally-transmitted music that has been out in the world, has been effected by the world, has come back and has begun to turn full circle again.'

Dylan plugs in

The transposition from pure traditional to a more rock-oriented music took place in the mid-1960s. Rock and folk both changed when Bob Dylan went electric at The Newport Folk Festival. Accused of betraying his folk roots and poisoning the music with electric guitars and drums, Dylan shrugged off the begrudgers and plugged into a music that managed to mix the plain, intelligent musings of folk with the muscularity of rock. Dylan has been credited with inventing a new species of music – folk rock – a cross-fertilisation that reverberates with a strong communicative power to this day.

ABOVE: *De Dannan have made several forays into rock music, but have always returned to their traditional Irish roots.*

In Ireland, this cultural resonance of the mid-1960s was picked up by a group called Sweeney's Men, perhaps the prototypical electric folk group. They formed in the West of Ireland in 1966, the original line-up being Andy Irvine, Joe Dolan and Johnny Moynihan, their initial intention to be a successful, traditional folk band. To this end they played in large country venues and dances, popularising their 'art' by meeting, and performing in front of, thousands of people. Their hard work and soft folk was greeted with appreciation, culminating in a number one single in 1967 with 'Old Maid In The Garrett'. Midway through 1967, Joe Dolan was replaced by Terry Woods, a consummate multi-instrumentalist with leanings toward American rather than Irish folk customs.

In 1968, Sweeney's Men released their eponymous debut album, a collection of archetypal folk songs. Following the album's release, Andy Irvine left the group and Ireland for Europe, only to be superseded by Henry McCullough, a Northern Irish electric guitarist whose experience with rock and psychedelic bands of the day (Eire Apparent being the most notable) gave him an enviable reputation among the Irish rock fraternity. The resulting combination of folk and rock lasted only several months and was never recorded.

Rocking folkies

Reports of their live shows of the time indicate that Sweeney's Men were on the cusp of creatively and commercially coalescing the two forms. It was not to be, however. McCullough went on to join English rough'n'blues singer Joe Cocker, while Woods and Moynihan carried on to record a second album that, although featuring a couple of songs which were co-written with McCullough ('A Mistake No Doubt' and 'Hall Of Mirrors'), failed to live up to the promise of a great idea. It was left to other groups (most notably Fairport Convention who effectively invented English folk rock) to take on the brief but crucial influences of Sweeney's Men. Early 1970s band Steeleye Span were particularly good exponents of this style.

Following the disbandment of Sweeney's Men, Terry Woods flirted with an Irish group by the name of Orphanage, a 'mixum-gatherum' conglomeration mainly made up of essentially travelling musicians with eclectic influences. Among the group's

> *'Yes, I suppose I do sweat too much!'*
>
> *CHRISTY MOORE.*

BELOW: *Both Andy Irvine (left) and Paul Brady began as folk musicians, but Brady later moved closer to rock.*

many members was a young black Irishman called Philip Lynott, who later went on to international acclaim as the frontman of Thin Lizzy. After a short hiatus, Terry and his wife, Gay, travelled to England where they eventually hitched up with Fairport Convention's ex-bass player, Ashley Hutchings, and an English folk duo, Maddy Prior and Tim Hart. Steeleye Span were born, releasing **Hark! The Village Wait** in 1970, an album that, although generally regarded as the first authoritative fusion of traditional folk with rock instruments, was released a year after Fairport Convention's groundbreaking **Liege And Lief**. Both releases, however, were equally influential.

Terry and Gay Woods went on to record in the guise of The Woodsband as well as under the more simple and straightforward title of Gay and Terry Woods. The Woodsband's self-titled debut album in 1971 is an assured and highly successful collection of songs that firmly established the duo as being at the forefront of a new breed of Irish musician. Their subsequent albums as a duo veered from the inventive to the inoffensive as the couple went through both personal and musical changes. They still

played rock music with a lyrical, rustic flavour but it was never to be as awe-inspiring. Gay Woods formed the extremely intelligent and boisterous Auto Da Fe in 1980 but has latterly taken on a low profile in the Irish music industry. Terry Woods joined The Pogues in the second half of the 1980s, a natural extension of his original vision.

Vision is a word that could equally be applied to Dr. Strangely Strange, a definite product of their times: the late 1960s. Their combination of folk, rock and a psychedelic 'whatever-you're-having-yourself' sense of experimentation ensured that they will always be looked upon as innovative but not largely influential. The core of the group – Ivan Pawle, Tim Goulding and Tim Booth – were archetypal student-hippies, associating themselves with the era's liberal attitudes and air of freedom in everything.

Dr. Strangely Strange certainly weren't rock'n'roll – at least not as we know it – but they undoubtedly provided an intriguing footnote in the annals of Irish rock. In contrast, both Tír Na nOg and Scullion profitably invested Irish folk rock with material of lyrical intensity and musical maturity. Tír Na nOg were essentially an

ABOVE: *After spending the 1970s making music in the folk rock mould, Gay Woods (in foreground) surprised the traditionalists by forming new wave outfit Auto Da Fe.*

acoustic duo (Sonny Condell and Leo O'Kelly) with a soft rock sensibility. They had moderate success abroad, their second and third albums, 1972's *Tear And A Smile* and 1973's *Strong In The Sun* consolidating their position as leaders of a sort in the acoustic rock tradition. Tír Na nOg split up in 1974 (although the duo briefly formed again in the late 1980s), O'Kelly concentrating on writing and Condell well into the concept of Scullion, another group working in a similar vein.

Acoustic excellence

The core personnel were Condell, Philip King and Greg Boland, all three contributing to the multifarious fund of folk rock oriented material. By no means integral to the internationalisation of Irish traditional-to-rock music – unlike, say, Thin Lizzy, Horslips, The Pogues and The Saw Doctors – Scullion have their place in Irish rock music history. Sonny Condell's songwriting contribution, for instance, cannot be ignored – many of his compositions on 1981's *Balance And Control* and 1983's *White Side Of Night* are state of the art, acoustic soft rock classics with a distinct Irish/Celtic flavour. Scullion are continually in the throes of breaking up and reforming, each time with different people, but latterly seem to have discovered a balance of sorts which indicates a seasoned maturity on the parts of the respective core members.

If any band broke new and commercial ground in the early 1970s – especially in the context of transforming such a conventional and almost ridiculously revered tradition as Irish folk into something else entirely – it was Horslips.

Part Irish folk traditionalists, part glam rock band, part chemical-crazed gang of five, Horslips were the answer to many an Irish teenager's prayers. Sick of being force-fed Irish traditional tunes from men with shaggy beards and woolly jumpers – and thoroughly excited by rock and pop groups beaming into their sitting rooms every Thursday evening on *Top Of The Pops* – the native Irish adolescent boys and girls were thrilled skinny at having their very first ethnic rock band. If Thin Lizzy were deemed to be that little bit too macho and hard rock oriented, then Horslips, with their satin and tat costumes and rocked-up jigs and reels fitted the teenager's identikit picture of shamrock'n'roll perfectly.

Formed in the early 1970s, the definitive line-up of Horslips was Jim Lockhart (keyboards, uilleann pipes, flute, vocals), Barry Devlin (bass guitar, vocals), Eamon Carr (drums, percussion), Charles O'Connor (violin, mandolin, vocals), and Johnny Fean (guitars, banjo). Fean was brought in to replace Declan Sinnott (who, in turn, had previously replaced Gus Guest, Horslips' guitarist for the first few months of their existence).

In early 1972, Horslips released their debut single, 'Johnny's Wedding', on their own independently set up label, Oats. It caused a cultural riot, its blending of heads down, no-nonsense rock instrumentation and traditional origins a potent combination. The song divided the populace. The hip youth of the day viewed the band as a necessary shot in the arm in pop culture terms. For them, traditional music was deemed to be too precious, too elitist and too old-fashioned for them to embrace with any degree of enthusiasm.

The new culture

During the early 1970s in Ireland, rock culture (both indigenous and Anglo/American) became an increasingly more important part of people's social and personal lives. Its attendant lifestyle of fashion, attitude and dress sense enabled Irish teenagers to select what they wanted to see and hear. Horslips, with all of their members then in their early 20s, were obviously youthful and experienced enough to realise this. Carr, Devlin and O'Connor all came from advertising backgrounds and had the prevailing trends at their fingertips.

The traditional establishment, on the other hand, looked upon the garishly dressed and long-haired group as a travesty. The purists of the day were cautious in their opinions and sceptical of Horslips' cultural aesthetic. Where the old guard completely underrated the band, however, was in their comprehension of both their traditional lineage and the medium of rock music as global communication. In 1972, Horslips released their debut album *Happy To Meet, Sorry To Part*, to internationally clamourous and positive reviews. They had arrived, the kids loved them and the traditional establishment could go whistle a tune on its flute for all they cared.

During their topsy-turvy 10-year career, Horslips released albums of varying strength and creativity. The follow up to their debut, *The Tain* (1973), a conceptual album that relates the Irish mythical story of ancient provincial battles, is now rightly regarded as one of the most important in Irish rock music.

LEFT: *The bright lights and glitzy outfits which were much in evidence at Horslips concerts couldn't disguise the fact that their finest music was based on their knowledge of traditional Irish music and culture.*

The album also contained 'Dearg Doom', the song that Horslips are perhaps best known for. A classic Celtic rock song that strides the boundaries of rock and folk, with its interweaving guitars and pipes, it is still played regularly on Irish radio and fondly remembered by every Irish rock fan born in the 1950s and 1960s.

Subsequent album releases were not as widely acclaimed or as commercially successful. *Dancehall Sweethearts* (1974) now sounds sorely dated, while both 1975's *The Unfortunate Cup Of Tea* – not so much inspired Celtic rock as bland, ordinary rock – and *Drive The Cold Winter Away* were lacklustre sidesteps in a previously glittering body of work. With record label and touring conflicts – the band had signed a distribution deal with RCA and were required to promote the product thereof – Horslips were suffering from creative and personal atrophy. Following a stop-gap live album in 1976 – the rough if tolerable *Horslips Live* – the band took time to recuperate from life on the road and set about recording a collection of interlinked, thematic songs that was to be their last great album.

The Book Of Invasions: A Celtic Symphony (1976) drew its strengths from the members' own deep-rooted knowledge of their country's heritage and history. Detailing the pre-Christian occupation of Ireland, Horslips triumphally merged mythology with a soft focussed and urbane lyrical stream of Celtic rock. The results were marvellous.

The long goodbye

From this album on, sadly, Horslips began suffering from internal and musical disagreements, which effectively meant that subsequent releases would not be as cohesive as their former glories. Their final trio of studio albums – *Aliens* (1977), *The Man Who Built America* (1978) and *Short Stories Tall Tales* (1979) – saw a group fractured by differing musical styles. A farewell live album, *The Belfast Gigs* (1980), bade a final, demonstrative goodbye to one of Ireland's most colourful, influential and successful groups.

During their decade together, Horslips entertained and educated with their forcefulness of character and their love of lore. There has been no band like them although

many groups of many nationalities have tried in vain to assimilate the unique Horslips sound; and this is even more true in the current climate of increasing accessibility to many world/ethnic musics. It's unlikely that there will ever be. The influence and legacy of Horslips remains untouched, their golden moments still shining through the years.

A new direction

If Horslips were an antidote to a peculiarly Irish malaise in the early 1970s – an Irish youth culture stifled by the twin guardians of conservatism and tradition – then The Pogues could be seen to be their natural 1980s equivalents. The key figure in The Pogues was Shane MacGowan who, in the early 1980s, formed the band around a disparate bunch of second generation Irishmen and one woman. MacGowan's musical background is as important as his genealogical one, and his experiences in the London punk wars as the frontman for The Nipple Erectors (later abbreviated to The Nips), were a major influence on his forming his major rhythmic *raison d'être* in relation to future projects.

In 1983, MacGowan – along with Spider Stacey (tin whistle), James Fearnley (accordion), Andrew Ranken (drums), Cait O'Riordan (electric bass), and Jem Finer (banjo) – began to sing his and other Irish rebel songs in a variety of London pub venues. Their technique of playing and structuring of songs was, at the time, quite unique and The Pogues can be credited with creating folk punk.

With MacGowan's punk textures and post-punk, crude but fervently literary lyrics, and the band's hell for leather playing style, The Pogues initially reached out to a partisan audience of dispossessed Irish expatriates. This soon changed with the release of their first album in 1984. *Red Roses For Me* comprises songs that are steeped in the *tradition* of Irish folk yet are executed with a compassionate resistance against the status quo. The Pogues took various styles of orthodox folk song interpretation and bent them entirely to their will with little regard as to how this would be received by the folkies. If the album shocked the folk purists – defined by Philip King as people 'who don't believe that the

> *'May I sound arrogant? We have originality and a love of life. God, that sounds arrogant and pretentious!'*
>
> SPIDER STACEY, THE POGUES.

music can go on somewhere else' – The Pogues' live shows were greeted with a mixture of massed acclaim and apoplexy. Their infamy spread far and wide and, eventually, they arrived in Ireland in the summer of 1985 to perform at an open-air festival. They played a stormer but, more crucially, met up with ex-Sweeney's Men member, Terry Woods, a man who helped form the field of folk-to-rock music. There was a mutual regard and empathy and Woods joined the band, as did the former Radiators From Space guitarist and co-vocalist, Philip Chevron.

Appearing to be more Irish than the Irish themselves, The Pogues later caused a furore when they appeared on an Irish radio talk/music show, in a one-sided conversation with die-hard traditionalists. Philip King recalls: 'Some people went bananas, including myself. I remember ringing a producer at the radio station when The Pogues were on the show, and having a ferocious row with him on the air, then meeting Phil Chevron a couple of weeks later in a bar, getting very drunk and sorting it all out.'

The band's detractors – and there were many in those early days – were forced to eat their words on the 1985 release of The Pogues' follow-up, **Rum, Sodomy And The Lash**. Shane MacGowan's exemplary and original songwriting technique was there for all to experience. Songs such as 'The Old Main Drag' and 'The Sick Bed Of Cuchulainn' both expressed a view of the Irish emigrant abroad that had rarely, if ever, been previously touched upon.

Yet it wasn't long before The Pogues began to venture out from their highly defined musical enclave: two EPs released in 1985 and 1986 showed the band to be as willing to experiment as they were to be casually shambolic. **Poguetry In Motion** (1985/1991) and **Haunted** (1986) saw The Pogues trying out, with varying degrees of success, different textural compositions. They also lost bassist O'Riordan around the time she married Elvis Costello (he produced the band's first single, 'A Pair Of Brown Eyes', and **Rum, Sodomy And The Lash**). Her replacement was a Pogues roadie, Daryl Hunt.

In the latter half of the 1980s, The Pogues combined with respected Irish ballad group, The Dubliners, on 'The Irish Rover' (1987), a popular Irish traditional ditty, and one that was performed in a suitably chaotic manner. In many ways, this was seen as The Pogues dutifully saluting their elders for their popularisation of Irish music internationally.

Falling stars

After this meeting of the clans, The Pogues' star began to fall from the ascendant. Although charting quite high – Top 5 – their final brace of albums in the 1980s (**If I Should Fall From Grace With God**, 1988, and **Peace And Love**, 1989) were greeted by a critical cold shoulder. A few gems were on each – in particular the magical 'Fairytale Of New York' on **If I Should...** – but overall the idea of The Pogues as a musically creative group was wearing thin.

There were a number of factors behind their decline, not least being the debilitating effect touring and alcohol intake was having on MacGowan. Live – always the preferable Pogues setting – the band were

becoming a grotesque parody of themselves, with a generally stupefied Shane hopelessly fronting a bunch of obviously embarrassed, if somewhat gung-ho, musicians. This wasn't to last. Following a compilation album released in late 1991 – the not quite aptly-named *The Best Of The Pogues* – MacGowan was asked to leave the band.

With his drinking problem causing muscular difficulties and blackouts, MacGowan seemed almost relieved to go. His place was taken over on a semi-permanent basis by ex-lead singer of prime time punk group The Clash, Joe Strummer. Because of contractual obligations, Strummer is a member of The Pogues in a stand-in capacity only, but from a live performance aspect he fits in fairly well. It is expected that Shane MacGowan will contribute songs to The Pogues' next album, as well as working on his own album.

The Pogues provide a skewed footnote to Irish rock music by virtue of their background and attitude. They simultaneously heralded a new approach to Irish folk whilst denouncing its antedeluvian posture. Although not as musically dogmatic as they were in their formative years, The Pogues – with or without Shane MacGowan – have in their ranks a number of other fine, but not as substantial, songwriters.

'The Pogues were a very healthy thing for Irish music,' says Philip King. 'What they did for Irish people who were smug in their attitudes was to give them a right dig.'

Another band to give people a 'right dig' are The Saw Doctors. Like Horslips and The Pogues before them, The Saw Doctors have divided opinion, albeit in a slightly more censorious manner. It all started for the group in the late 1970s in Tuam, County Galway, when Davy Carton and Leo Moran founded a punk band, Blaze X, and wrote songs as clichéd and derivative as any other second division punk group of the day. Enjoyable but not essential, Blaze X petered out, and so did the members' respective musical careers.

Unlikely doctors

Fast forward to the mid-1980s when a bunch of likely lads – featuring Moran and Carton among them – formed The Saw Doctors. Their debut single, 'N17', was produced by new County Galway resident and Irish music enthusiast Mike Scott of The Waterboys, but it did nothing to endear the band to the hearts of the record buying public. The follow up was an adaptation of an old Blaze X song, the chorus of which had been around for approximately 10 years, and the lyrics for about three.

ABOVE: *After Shane MacGowan's departure from The Pogues, he was replaced by former Clash frontman Joe Strummer for the band's next tour.*

The song was called 'I Useta Love Her' and it catapulted The Saw Doctors to national fame. Released at the end of 1990, it carried on into 1991, swelling interest in the band's debut album, *If This Is Rock And Roll I Want My Old Job Back*, a collection of self-composed, derivative tunes that mixed some bold, swaggering hand-me-down rock with the charm and rusticity of traditional music. The album is a hackneyed effort – rambling trad tunes jigged up with guitars, bass and drums – but it struck profound chords, both negative and positive, in the psyche of the Irish nation.

Split opinion

The schools of thought on the band are, generally speaking, of two kinds. The first is that they are the best Irish band to have emerged in years and that their traditionally-rooted rock'n'roll is speaking out to the nation's geographically disadvantaged; that their songs of country charm and humour, with their offbeat sentiment and bucolic sympathies, are related to mostly by those weary of sophisticated, so-called 'modern' music; that the band are indigenous rock'n'roll spokespersons for *all* generations – loved by the kids (who snigger at the crude parts in the songs), laughed at by the over 50s (who think of the band members

as fine young healthy lads singing songs about fine young healthy lasses) and praised by the critics (who view the band's songs of callow, lust-filled men, idealistic emigrants and flagrantly opportunistic young bucks as being a perfect antidote to the apparent seriousness of the vast majority of modern Irish rock groups). The second school of thought is that The Saw Doctors are by far the worst Irish rock band to have emerged in years; that they are dragging Irish rock music and its attendant culture back by about 10 years and giving non-Irish people the distinct impression that their subspecies of Celtic rock music – an epicene compound of The Clash, Horslips, The Waterboys, The Pogues and Bruce Springsteen – is all that Ireland currently has to offer the world. Typically, The Saw Doctors, with their collective down-to-earth demeanour, have dismissed such theorising as rubbish. That stance hasn't prevented leading Irish newspaper columnists and social commentators from holding forth on the national importance of the group.

The band, on the other hand, feel that their contribution to Irish rock music has been – and will continue to be – a sense of nostalgia, both musically and sociologically. Says lead singer Davy Carton: 'We brought the '60s feel back into (Irish) music again. Music was getting very serious, people were getting very wrapped up in themselves. Young men, if they didn't make it, would get uptight. Enjoy yourselves, for God's sake, is what we say; bring the sunshine back into the music.'

They also see themselves as being the band to fuse traditional with rock. Davy Carton again: 'We'd be seen to be doing that. We are an Irish rock'n'roll band. How many avenues can you explore? People talk of Horslips and compare us to The Pogues, but we're not like The Pogues at all. We are, perhaps, from another branch...' Increasingly, the 'other branch' aesthetic is gaining both in credence and popularity. Aside from the several main instigators who are mentioned here – those bands who have undoubtedly used traditional Irish music to their own ends and visions, the *auteur* Irish rock groups – there are some other notable figures in and out of Irish rock music who have engaged themselves in cross-fertilisation techniques. Van Morrison is, perhaps, the most obvious example. To a certain degree, he has refined his neo-religious vision of artistic transcendence to a recognisable if somewhat ambiguous point.

The starting point of Morrison's growing awareness of his birthplace is with his 1974 album ***Veedon Fleece***, a brooding collection of nebulous, remote songs that,

> *'We really are more important than U2 and Sinead (O'Connor)! And we tell better stories than they do! Did I ever tell you the one about the wandering tin whistle?'*
>
> PADDY MALONEY, THE CHIEFTAINS.

LEFT: *Despite the psychedelic background, The Saw Doctors look more like traditional Irish musicians than flamboyant rockers.*

ABOVE: *Traditional Irish band The Chieftains. In 1988, Van Morrison paid tribute to his roots by recording the album* Irish Heartbeat *with them.*

paradoxically, touch pertinently upon his fervent reactions to Celticism. If subsequent albums such as 1979's *Into The Music* and 1980's *Common One* see him playing around with both the structure of rock and the Irish dimension of the abstract mood-song, it was on 1982's *Beautiful Vision* and 1983's *Inarticulate Speech Of The Heart* that he captured in all its wonderment and breadth the magnitude and scope of his own brand of rock-fuelled traditional music.

Since then, Morrison has continued to regularly release albums – the culmination of which is 1988's *Irish Heartbeat*, his collaboration with supreme Irish traditional ensemble, The Chieftains – that encapsulate the (so-called) Irish mystical spirit and his seemingly never-ending quest to express his almost tangible spirituality. One thing remains definite, however, and that is Van Morrison's inestimable and constant rein-

forcement of Irish rock music as an elemental, yet sturdy, art form.

If anybody has taken on the Morrison mantle (albeit by attempting to correlate an indefinable mysticism with an avant-garde sensibility) it's Pierce Turner. Wexford-born but culturally bred in New York, Turner has, in the space of a mere handful of albums, rigorously defined the meaning of the term 'New Age'; not in the ridiculed, contemptible manner, but in the exploratory, expansive sense. Turner's most recent album, *Now Is Heaven* (1991), even has a tribute to Morrison with a rap on his cover version of 'Here Comes The Night'.

Turner's creative aspirations, however, are not as clear as some Irish critics might like to think. The same could be said of U2, whose contribution to Irish rock is as undeniable as it is essential. Their scant sponsorship of Irish-imbued rock music, however,

can be explained by their members' respective backgrounds and influences. Although they used the Irish language title of 'An Cat Dubh' (The Black Cat) on their debut album, *Boy* (1980), and employed traditional musicians Vinnie Kilduff (uilleann pipes) and Steve Wickham (fiddle) on a couple of tracks on their follow-up, *October* (1981), it could be argued that U2 crystallise the essence of the Irish rather than the music.

The sole exceptions to this are The Edge's composition on *Rattle And Hum* (1988), 'Van Dieman's Land' – a compelling, droning ballad that slots uncomfortably into the spirited eclecticism of that double album – and Bono's unaccompanied singing of the self-composed ballad/lament, 'My Wild Irish Rose' on the BBC documentary series, *Bringing It All Back Home*.

On Bono's involvement in that series, Philip King says, 'As to whether Bono will continue writing in a balladic form, I don't know. What he does, he does. He doesn't do things just for the sake of it.' Time will tell, although, in a tangential way, time has already told, certainly if you take into consideration Bono's musical involvement with Clannad on the 1986 (later re-released in 1989) single 'In A Lifetime', where his breathy vocal interweaves with that of the band's lead singer, Maire Ni Bhraonain. It seems that, like his group, Bono has a communicable Irish aesthetic, but as to whether this will eventually be transferred into a recurring musical form is anybody's guess.

Clannad themselves have also done their bit for the internationalisation of Irish rock music, even if their Donegal traditional origins have been swapped for a package of banked keyboards and quasi-ethereal tunes. Curiously, Clannad's position as purveyors of pristine, traditionally-based songs and instrumentals has been superseded by an erstwhile band member, Maire's sister, Eithne Ni Bhraonain. Although better known as Enya, this younger sibling has, since *Watermark* (1988), cut a swathe through New Age electronics/ethnic/world musics to an extent where both style and – albeit to a lesser degree – content are of paramount importance.

Exported sounds

Thus, Enya and her integral team of producer and lyricist (Nicky and Roma Ryan), choose to present Irish music as both profoundly melancholic and not too exciting. This cannot be said for the myriad amount of non-Irish artists and groups who – from the early 1980s onwards – have unashamedly borrowed from Irish traditional music to inform and enhance their art.

So what do Elvis Costello, Kate Bush, The Waterboys, John Cage, Kirsty MacColl, John Lydon, Dexy's Midnight Runners and The Wonder Stuff all have in common? At one time or another, they've skilfully appropriated the fabric of Irish traditional music. They've mutated it into something that sounds like their own; even

ABOVE: *The latest production techniques are used on Clannad's albums to highlight Maire Brennan's delicate voice, but the band also enjoy getting back to basics.*

if the end results are as diverse as Kate Bush's implementation of pipes (Liam O'Flynn) and fiddle (Sean Keane) on 'Night Of The Swallow' from the *The Dreaming* (1982) or John Lydon's rhythmically Irish refrain of 'May the road rise with you' on Public Image Limited's single 'Rise' (1986).

Similarly, both The Wonder Stuff and Kirsty MacColl have integrated Irish influences on their respective albums – *Never Loved Elvis* (1991) and *Electric Landlady* (1991) – to the point where they fit in seamlessly with other musical styles. Avant-garde composer John Cage, has taken the entire process a step further and has conceptualised a piece of traditional noise titled 'Roaratorio'. Modelled on a James Joyce book – *Finnegan's Wake* – Cage has formulated a work of non-art music whereby he intones improvisational word associations from the text of the book while six traditional musicians each play their own choice of traditional music for no longer than 20 minutes. 'Roaratorio' hasn't often been performed...

So where does this leave Irish traditional music in the 1990s? The possibilities appear to be almost endless. For 10 years now, the dividing lines between various areas of music have been crossed, and have become blurred into something of an indefinable whole. If the music is to survive, this will have to continue until eventually the lines disappear altogether. 'The lines don't matter,' says Philip King. 'Pigeon-holing is done by critics and record companies. The music industry can call it what it wants – the music is out there. If the record companies want to fuck around with it, paint it a different colour and call it something else, then fine, but it won't go away, that's for sure.'

> '*My music doesn't have a love song that cries out "love me, baby, love me". What it has is a melody which will go into your emotion and stir up something from within*'
>
> *ENYA.*

RIGHT: *Ex-Sex Pistol John Lydon was one of the most surprising of several British rockers who looked to Irish music for inspiration and ideas.*

ON THE FRINGE

'I'd rather be Philip Glass than Van Morrison.'

– PIERCE TURNER.

IT'S SOMEWHAT DIFFICULT TO THINK OF the avant-garde in an Irish context, mainly because the overriding mood and mien of Irish music is rigidly rock and pop oriented. Most Irish groups and bands – from those of the 1960s indigenous beat boom to the 1990s internationalist rock stylists – have taken their influences from within acceptable and undemanding parameters. With few exceptions – detailed further on – the face of Irish rock has been, is, and will undoubtedly continue to be, rather one dimensional. Very enjoyable, often inspirational, occasionally exciting, but generally lacking the innate thrilling adventurism and possibility of failure of many American or British avant-gardists.

Of course, the 1990s are aeons away from the 1960s and 1970s with regard to the artist's approach toward application and execution. Contemporary Irish artists such as Gavin Friday, Pierce Turner and U2 have used elements of exploratory musics in their generally successful attempts at fusing the offbeat with the mainstream. Back in the pre-punk 1970s days, Ireland was awash with the last vestiges of showbands, and with the rise of Irish rock music as a reputable and viable international proposition, there was almost no apparent interest in music experimentation.

Historically, this period of time was crucial not only for Irish experimentalists but also for Irish rock music. Come the summer of 1975, the Irish music industry was rocked to its foundations by the tragic killing of several members of one of Ireland's foremost bands, The Miami Showband. Immediately, all international visiting acts cancelled their proposed gigs in the country, and the situation was not fully rectified until the late 1970s. This, ironically, allowed homegrown acts to attain a higher profile – promoters couldn't put on any concerts

LEFT: *Gavin Friday and The Man Seezer, back-to-back in typical art-pop mode.*

unless Irish acts were on the bill. Thus were sown the seeds for an unheralded growth in orthodox Irish rock groups.

With Thin Lizzy, Horslips and solo artists such as Van Morrison and Rory Gallagher making their respective marks outside Ireland – and the large number of at-home, low profile rock bands sweating to emulate this success – the idea of experimenting with music structures and shapes wasn't exactly a widespread one. Consequently, Irish teenagers and people forming groups now take as the norm that their methods of expression and communication will be restricted to rock'n'roll or pop. It wasn't always like that…

In Ireland in the late 1960s/early 1970s, the counter-culture was as much a part of student body activity as it was anywhere else in the world. In the freedom of expression ethic (or megalomaniacal self-indulgence in a number of cases) of the times, several Irish ensembles were set up in defiance of the pop norm. Free-floating bands such as Tara Telephone, Mellow Candle, Supply Demand And Curve, Naïma and, surprise, surprise, very early Thin Lizzy, experimented with various combinations of poetry, music, and free-form jazz/rock fusion.

The spiritual element

Naïma – their name is taken from a John McLaughlin and Carlos Santana album, *Love, Devotion, Surrender* (1973) and is also the name of John Coltrane's wife – were a fusion group of that time. Garvan Gallagher, now part of Irish folk songstress Mary Black's musical entourage, was a member of Naïma and was also integral to Supply Demand And Curve. He remembers the nature of this experimental group: 'In an Irish context, I suppose we were avant-garde. We tried to retain a spiritual element of The Mahavishnu Orchestra, although we weren't devotees of any particular cult or guru. We felt that musical excellence and hard work were important in a spiritual as well as in an ethical sense.'

Kieran Owens is an influential group manager of largely Irish acts (he managed The Virgin Prunes for over four years and is currently in charge of Hinterland, Sack, and Katell Keinig). In the late 1960s, he was an active observer of the burgeoning counter-culture scene. He recalls those early days: 'All these people were very much musos, really living the lifestyle of counter-culture, Timothy Leary, hippie, drop-out… They were very much affected by the student riots

in Paris and the events in Vietnam. Bands like Mellow Candle were part of that whole Dublin Southside hippy commune.'

The city centre hub of activity for these groups and their supporters was The Project Arts Centre, one of Ireland's most innovative and supportive arts administrations. Along with The Project, Dublin's Trinity College and other centres of student activity became support networks where, as Kieran Owens recollects, 'the very radical left politics combined with an immense supply of drugs and a booming economy to allow this scene to flourish.' The overall impression one receives from Kieran is that this, like every scene, had its own set of semi-elitist rules. 'If you weren't hanging out at The Project and listening to all that stuff and being incredibly hip – read gauche – then you were just some kind of Neanderthal. It was a pretty tight, bigoted community of aesthetes.' Nevertheless, this wilful spirit of many like-minded individuals to express themselves laid down the stepping stones which would lead to further creativity, although not necessarily in the avant-garde field.

Most of the participants of the experimental era went on to greater things – Thin Lizzy to crack the world; Eamon Carr (from Tara Telephone) to Horslips, record production and rock journalism; Andrew Boland and Brian Masterson (from Naïma and Supply Demand And Curve, respectively), to studio production work. Many eschewed their former avant-garde musical activities for a rather more sedentary and less wayward life. There were, however, exceptions to the rule.

New horizons

The two most obvious are Jolyon Jackson and Roger Doyle. Jackson became musically involved with Doyle whilst studying at Trinity College during the late 1960s. There they both worked with Supply Demand And Curve, and Jazz Therapy, two of Ireland's most individualistic and experimental outfits. Following these demanding associations, Jackson moved into contemporary theatre, experimenting with dance and music and working on soundtracks that inexhaustably delved into the vast well of unclassifiable music. Sadly, Jackson died in 1985 from Hodgkin's Disease – but his contribution to the avant-garde is substantial.

It's generally recognised that Roger Doyle was the first to deviate from the established and approved route into Irish rock music. Throughout the 1970s and

1980s, Doyle countered the standard practices of what music should and could be, culminating in a sequence of albums and film soundtracks that are as beautiful as they are bold.

Born in Dublin in 1949, Doyle's musical education began as a child when his parents decided to send him to classical piano lessons. Come his teens, Doyle transferred his classical leanings to a rock context when he played drums in a local amateur beat group, The Malabeats.

It wasn't until a couple of years later that Doyle found a rather more conducive resting home in Supply Demand And Curve, and Jazz Therapy. The former band, in particular, fused jazz, rock, folk and classical musics in such a way as to demand attention rather than shun it. Following two years with Supply Demand And Curve and some international touring, he left the looseness and unconstraining nature of the group for the more pensive world of music study. By the mid-1970s, Doyle had secured a scholarship at The Hague's Royal University of Music.

Album releases from Roger Doyle are few and far between. His debut album, the self-financed *Ozzio No* (1975) is what the average music listener would call unlistenable. This argument aside, it predates the 1980s and 1990s technological concepts of samples and bite sounds by almost 10 years. It wasn't that the unconventional approach utilised by Doyle and his partners (Jolyon Jackson, cello, and Brian Dunning, flute) was in any way new; as a disciple of both American John Cage and Frenchman Pierre Henri, Doyle knew where his heart and influences lay at this time. The important thing was that no one from Ireland was doing anything of this kind. That made the admittedly rarely heard album such a great challenge and triumph.

RIGHT: *Roger Doyle, usually to be found on a completely different wavelength to other musicians.*

After studying at The Hague, Doyle moved to Utrecht's Institute of Sonology, where he developed a piece of music called 'Solar Eyes', an almost Doppler Effect soundscape of sonar bleeps and hisses, where the John Cage concepts of the equal importance of sound and silence were accentuated. Doyle then spent some time in Helsinki's Experimental Radio Music Centre where he obtained the chance to broadcast this piece of sonar dub music twice, both backwards and forwards! Could anyone really tell the difference? His second album, *Thalia* (1978), featured 'Solar Eyes' and other innovative musical pieces.

Come 1981, following working periods in Holland, Ireland and Finland, Doyle formed – with Irish actress Olwen Fouere – his own theatre music group, Operating Theatre. Aptly named, they sliced conventional ideas of music and performance apart, leaving in their wake a sequence of rigidly avant-garde pieces that were as discordant as they were stimulating. *Rapid Eye Movements* (1981) included these compositions. Operating Theatre's follow-up album, *Miss Mauger* (1983), showed Doyle to be moving away from the dissonant methods of his previous musical works towards a much more ambient framework where undulating rhythms waved and ruled.

Over the next three years, Doyle invested his compositional strengths and his leanings towards the peculiarly English post-punk minimalist sounds of bands such as Clock DVA, This Heat and Cabaret Voltaire. Aware of the creative possibilities that such a move could open up, he began to introduce warped rock elements into his music. Thus began the accessibility of his music to such an extent that U2's Bono offered Doyle the opportunity to record and release material through U2's then recently initiated Mother label. *Spring Is Coming* (1986) – an altogether other-worldly and highly commendable mixture of rock/opera/classical/ethnic musics – was the result of Bono's perceptive, enthusiastic interaction and Doyle's increasingly non-avant-garde methodology.

Since then, Doyle has almost surreptitiously carried on his art in the guises of stage and soundtrack composer. The most successful venture was his elegaic work on Bob Quinn's 1988 silent film, *Buddawanny*, while his background musical work for the Gate Theatre's production of Oscar Wilde's *Salome* was equally acclaimed.

Like a number of people who have, so to speak, cut their teeth on an intellectual, academic edge, Doyle has succeeded in craftily combining the cerebral image of the

BELOW: *Operating Theatre always tried to open up as many creative avenues as possible.*

humourless avant-garde with the excitement of rock music. It's difficult to know exactly where Roger Doyle fits into Irish music in the 1990s (certainly not as much as he fitted into the form in the 1970s), mainly because he has latterly maintained such a low commercial musical profile.

The onslaught of punk rock and its associated shattering of the concept of adept musicianship broke down more barriers than people thought it would. With its intrinsic attitude of do-it-yourself learning techniques, punk brought back natural minimalism and amateur experimentation. Known as non-musicians, a large number of performers – or people who thought they wanted to be performers – took to the stage and impro-

vised sonic attacks, recited poetry over droning electronic passages and generally created an atmosphere of alienation and aloofness. Certainly there was little of celebration in this formless music, even if it was created out of a will to 'kick against the pricks'. Prominent among such instigators is Stano.

Born in 1960 on the Northside of Dublin, John Stanley eventually became known as Stano via his schoolboy nicknames. Following a reasonably fractious upbringing, Stano caught the punk bug in the late 1970s, and through his first band, The Threat, released a typically angst-ridden debut single, 'Lullaby In C' (1980).

When The Threat broke up shortly after, Stano took time off from his day job

'Half my friends think what I do is crap. The other half think I'm mad'

STANO.

RIGHT: *Stano, adrift, windswept, interesting, and at the very edge of non-music possibilities.*

– carpentry – to experiment with *musique concréte*: common sound sources like people coughing, breaking glass, laughing, radio snippets, and the like. He'd also been writing his own form of poetry, so combining the two made an interesting if not wholly listenable collage of sound-noise.

The fruits of Stano's labours resulted in his debut solo release with 'Room' (1982), a single that afforded him a reputable cult status in Ireland. His debut solo album, **Content To Write In I Dine Weathercraft** (1983; re-issued in 1986) widened this cult status, being as it was a multifarious collection of 11 songs enveloped in not-so-typical sound structures. In other words, there was more variation and proficiency on the album than Stano's detractors had given him credit for. Helping him out on some of the tracks were female vocalist Suzanne Rattigan, bassist and one-time Van Morrison sidekick Jerome Rimson, and Roger Doyle. Reactions to the album inevitably ranged from the positive to the negative. Few people bought it, though, that's for sure…

Towards chaos

Stano's second album (recorded in 1984 but not released for two years), the equally abstrusely-named **Seducing Decadence In Morning Treecrash** (1986), was more harsh than his debut. Industrial in thought and deed, the album veered dangerously close to something beyond mayhem and disorder. There are vicious slashes of sound, jagged edges of askew guitar and an abstract interlinking of ethnic musics for good measure. The result is one of aural dislocation and far too atonal for its own good.

Following stints in London in the mid-1980s, Stano returned to Dublin where he discovered his profile had risen and that his music was being taken more seriously. (This led to the eventual release of **Seducing…**). It also paved the way for his third album, **Daphne Will Be Born Again** (1987), an instrumental album that, even from the title alone, reflected a normalcy that his work had previously lacked. There was also an upsurge of optimism within the music and song titles that indicated a person more at peace with himself. Stano was maturing both as a person and as a musician – the latter due in no small part to his acquaintanceship with the Fairlight computer.

Subsequent releases have proved to be equally positive and assured. Stano – like his avant-garde predecessor, Roger Doyle – found a working respite in Mother records

when the label decided to release **Only** (1989). An album of polar opposites and emotional responses, the track titles ('When Life Slips Away', 'Sweet Disposition', 'Wreckage') hint at the dichotomy within its creator. **Only** remains Stano's best album to date by virtue of its begrudging accessibility. His most recent recorded material shows no complacency or compromise. Now with a bunch of floating musicians – their group name, Wreckage, taken from the **Only** album – the release of their debut single, 'Morning' (1991), saw Stano take on a more rock-oriented stance with respect to his avant-garde leanings, making the song far more intriguing than one steeped in archetypal rock codes.

Essentially a performer who makes music out of a sense of necessity rather than fiscal needs, Stano's forthrightness and stubborness have proven to be both his freedom and strait-jacket. Not one to be bound by the crass ego gratification and financial reward of commercial success, Stano treads a solitary and idiosyncratic path. His music will, most probably, always be the preserve of those who tend to favour experimentation over formula.

Formulaic isn't the word that one would use to describe the brief recorded output and Irish arts support of performance artist Nigel Rolfe. An Englishman, Rolfe came to Ireland from Bath (where he had minor success with a couple of rock bands in the mid-1970s) and proceeded to focus his art forms onto a radical output.

Mind games

Involved with The Project Arts Centre, Rolfe was able to utilise his intellectual vocabulary to enable the right kind of contextual justification for putting on an event such as Dark Space, a 24-hour punk rock/performance festival held at The Project in the late 1970s. In this context, Rolfe was seen to be a crucial factor in the development of experimental art. His arts and administrative abilities allowed access to venue space, while the intellectual assistance he provided to musicians and other artists was, to put it mildly, welcomed.

Previously, Rolfe had been described simply as a moving sculpture. For this art form to work effectively, Rolfe felt he had to bring into his performances both the visual and the aural. This performance art gave way in the early 1980s to working with video and sound to accompany his extremist artistic vision. Using the burgeoning electronic music talents of keyboardist Steve

Belton and guitarist Pat O'Donnell (later this duo became better known as The Fountainhead), Rolfe created a multi-media performance art of staggering individuality and radicalism.

He soon dispensed with the services of these musicians and concentrated on writing his own material – based around his mid-1980s multi-media performance art work, *Island Stories* – of structurally tight, electronically-derived music. **Island Stories** (1986), the resulting album, contains sounds as diverse as those of household vacuum cleaners, brass instruments, electronically treated kotos, traditionally-based Irish laments (with the help, incidentally, of one Christy Moore), some choral music and ambient Celticisms. With no further important music releases in the pipeline, Nigel Rolfe continues to concentrate on his performance arts. His erstwhile contribution is underestimated and poorly documented.

Equally underestimated is the work of Ireland's most (read: only) extremist avant-garde group, The Virgin Prunes. The most reliable and exciting line-up of the band

was: Gavin Friday and Guggi (vocals/performers), Dave-Id (singer/performer), Haa Lacka Binttii (drums/keyboards), Dik Prune (guitar), and Strongman (bass). Binttii was later replaced by Mary D'Nellon – a man – who, in turn, was replaced by the original drummer, Pod.

If punk rock did anything positive, it was the opening up of possibilities for artistic creativity and expression. Punk hit Ireland later rather than sooner. As with glam rock, punk only held an Irish handful in its grasp. With The Radiators From Space being the sole Irish prototype for punk (The Boomtown Rats? Too old and too pop-oriented), it was left to a couple of groups with the tenets of British punk firmly in their thoughts to carry the torch. Enter U2 and, as mentioned above, The Virgin Prunes...

From their beginnings, both of these bands were inextricably linked by their association in what they themselves called Lypton Village. A curious mind game, Lypton Village was, according to Kieran Owens, 'a quirky, almost pseudo-Masonic association of language and gesture.' In other words, it was a very private world where its inhabitants could communicate only with each other, and where these communications would be coded specifically so that outsiders couldn't know what was being talked about.

Everyone in Lypton Village had their own names – Paul Hewson became Bono Vox, Dave Evans became The Edge, Fionnáin Hanvey became Gavin Friday, Derek Rowan became Guggi, and Dave Scott became Dave-Id Busarus. Other Village names included Pod and Strongman. Although both U2 and The Virgin Prunes were friends, their musical paths were at polar opposites. While U2 commenced their upwardly linear trajectory to worldwide fame through a sequence of startling and shrewd rockist movements, The Virgin Prunes began their scaling of rock's treacherous walls by an altogether more radical, surreal route. Equally determined to go their own way were Paranoid Visions, a punk band who have, throughout the past decade and a half, stubbornly ignored passing trends and fashions.

The Virgin Prunes took as their brief the re-creation on stage of Dadaist performance art principles. Allied to this was the Prunes'

LEFT: *Stubborn, blunt, and studiously uncommercial, Paranoid Visions are Ireland's ultimate punk rock idealists.*

music, a jarring, challenging amalgam of perverse virtuoso guitar work (courtesy of Dik Prune, otherwise known as Dick Evans, The Edge's brother) and an involuntary flexing of disharmonic rock-noise. The band formed in 1978, their first gig supporting The Clash at Dun Laoghaire's Top Hat, one of the country's major rock venues.

> ## 'I'm an acquired taste'
>
> ### GAVIN FRIDAY.

Not many people had even heard of The Virgin Prunes at this stage, but by the end of the night their name was on everyone's lips. The noise and performance of that night – Gavin Friday and Guggi, the two frontmen, had simulated sexual intercourse; Gavin split his trousers *à la* P.J. Proby, revealing his genitals and not being too shy about it – indicated that a new and shocking culture had just been born. You could say that Ireland wasn't really ready for it.

'The Virgin Prunes,' recounts ex-leader and schemer Gavin Friday, 'were going on about sex, love, betrayal, lust and death in a very schizophrenic, histrionic, rhetorical, wonderfully mad way. Ireland never experienced glam rock, sexuality in a 1970s ambiguous way, or the avant-garde, and The Virgin Prunes were all of that in one big explosion.'

As with punk in Britain and the USA, and with no precedents in Ireland, The Virgin Prunes violated the old school of entertainment values and performer-related virtues. Gavin Friday and his band of wily interpreters took the original aesthetics of punk extremely seriously. 'It was like "express yourself",' observes Gavin, 'and if you have to bring a pig's head on stage to do that, then fine. When Johnny Rotten said "don't dress like me", I took that for Bible. So I decided not to have yellow hair or a pin stuck through my nose. Instead, I'd have a four yard skirt and look like Rasputin on speed.'

Dressing up

If anything outraged the average Irish citizen, it was The Virgin Prunes' attempts at cross-dressing and their flouting of traditional and stereotypical attitudes towards sexuality. Along with the Prunes' baying-at-the-moon approach towards Irish politics and social values, Friday and his assorted pals were screaming aloud at every Irish cliché that annoyed them, particularly sexual categorisation.

This stance had its origins in Friday's teenage sexual awakenings. 'I was a very quiet boy at school, believe it or not. I was very shy, very gentle; I idolised Marc Bolan and wanted to look like him, so I grew my hair very long, got my ears pierced, and wore clothes the way I wanted to. I was finding out who I was in a sexual way, and suddenly a boot was on my head saying, "You are a poof". I was 12 years old and I didn't even know what the word meant. I know my sexuality now, but at that very early age my sexuality was being told to me by other people. I'm not gay, but I have a side that I'm not afraid of.'

This aspect of The Virgin Prunes was central to their beliefs and aesthetics, especially to Friday, who confesses to being the ringmaster of the entire Prunes spectacle. 'The most macho person in the group, Guggi, was the most effeminate looking. He looked like an androgynous angel meets David Bowie, and he was a lad, a humourous, straightforward guy, but he liked ambiguousness.'

A bizarre mixture

During the late 1970s, The Virgin Prunes' performances took on all the aspects of blood letting, Grand Guignol shock treatment. Like a spectral combination of Hieronymus Bosch, The Bay City Rollers and road drills, they increasingly relied more on mixed media events to get their ideas across to the Irish public than on rock-type 'gigs'. Their early 1980s performances – dubbed *A New Form Of Beauty* – in Dublin's Douglas Hyde Gallery were heralded and castigated in equal amounts.

With these events – atrocity exhibition meets savage, rural expressiveness – The Virgin Prunes overtly commented on the *naiveté* of Irish rock music's usual cosy relationship with its audience. It was a *tour de force* and, for many, the apogee of the band's carefully rehearsed primitivism.

'I was very angry and passionate about what I wanted to do,' recalls Friday. 'The masterminds behind the shock aesthetic of the Prunes were me and Dik. He was, and still is, a very talented guitarist. When I first met him he could play the Steve Howe guitar parts on Yes's *Close To The Edge* backwards! Why? Because he'd gotten bored playing them the normal way. Dik was a surreal Robert Fripp, so each gig, therefore, had to be different, a confrontation. I don't think we wanted to shock, we wanted to make people aware, to make them think.'

Musically, The Virgin Prunes challenged the listener as much as their live shows provoked the viewer. Their recorded output is as mixed as anything you care to consider. From 1981 to 1987, they released a dozen singles and five albums. Their debut single consisted of 'Twenty Tens'/'Revenge'/'I Hear The Children Crying' (1981), three songs that stated the Prunes' manifesto of continual change and conflict with startling assurance. On 'I Hear The Children Crying', Dave-Id intoned U2's '11 o'Clock Tick Tock' in a mocking, lugubrious way. Was this a joke? No one really knew for sure, perhaps least of all The Virgin Prunes.

Following their second single, 'In The Greylight', (1981), the band released a triptych of sound-noise/pop singles that remain their recorded peak. 'A New Form Of Beauty 1, 2, 3' (1981) came in, respectively, 7", 10" and 12" formats, and essentially reflected the Prunes' intellectual and primordial dissertations on a variety of subjects, most notably society's attitudes to mental dysfunction, primitivism, and subterranean consciousness.

In relation to mental instability, The Virgin Prunes, particularly Gavin Friday, bestowed the generosity of patronage towards several people who, by clinical standards at least, could be seen to be mentally abnormal. This stance was misinterpreted by many, who saw the group as deliberately perverting the normal course of events in these people's lives, quite possibly for their own deviant sense of humour. Active Virgin Prune member Dave-Id contracted meningitis at an early age and as a result he became severely mentally underdeveloped. There are several reasons behind the band's lending a helping hand toward Dave-Id – and, latterly, Gavin Friday's association with Aidan Walsh. It is possible that their various religious backgrounds – Gavin's upbringing was Roman Catholic; Guggi and Strongman's was strictly Protestant Fundamentalist; while their close friend Bono was involved in the Christian Shalom sect – engendered a kind of secular religious community that sought to befriend the handicapped.

Kieran Owens: 'Somewhere in there was a genuine – and I believe it was genuine – feeling of having someone as disadvantaged as Dave-Id and taking him out of himself. It was the best form of therapy he could

ever have had. He was accepted by the other members as an equal, because they were as weird as he was – or maybe they wanted to be as weird as Dave was! Through Dave-Id's own intellectual development, or where his mind went down so many different routes, the rest were able to follow. In a funny way, Dave-Id was always the real wild card of The Virgin Prunes. The rest of it could have been fabricated but with Dave-Id you never, ever, knew.'

> ***'Elvis is dead.***
> ***Now I take over'***
>
> AIDAN WALSH.

Touring Europe followed, the Prunes bringing their exceptional notion of catharsis to the English, French and Dutch. The response was pretty much the same – even the unflappable English rock audiences were gobsmacked by the band's methods of self-expression. More singles followed: 'Pagan Love Song', 'Baby Turns Blue' and 'The Faculties Of The Broken Heart' (all 1982), are fine examples of unnatural, prismatic pop songs. A debut album, *If I Die, I Die* (1982), was released to somewhat muted critical appraisal.

Sound without vision

Without the stage visuals, though, some of the songs lost their impact, a critical assessment that was to taunt the band up to their split in the mid-1980s. 'There was an element of entertainment there, as there always is,' observes Gavin, 'and that's what killed The Virgin Prunes, because we put up those confrontational barriers in front of us all the time. Clichés come in – you pull out the old pig's head and the dress. Some of the band started getting too competent and The Virgin Prunes could never be that. Some people started getting used to everything and other people started to want careers, and it just fell in on itself.'

A final studio album was released, *The Moon Looked Down And Laughed* (1986), a wide-ranging, idiosyncratic album and one that was far removed from their earlier material. A live album, *The Hidden Lie* (1987) was the final reminder of The Virgin Prunes' artistry.

Gavin isn't surprised that no one person or band has felt willing to take up the mantle laid down by The Virgin Prunes. 'The Virgin Prunes were a very political band, in that in 1980 we were dealing, in songs, about abortion, sexuality, surrealism, Dada and literature with both passion and intensity. But then, what is Ireland? It's a very

RIGHT: *Communing with Mother Earth and getting their hands dirty had great appeal for The Virgin Prunes.*

easygoing place. The Waterboys make more sense in Ireland, because people like their pint, their bit of blow and a bit of a vibe. They don't want to be hearing Prunes' songs. The Prunes looked to Europe – I still do – while about 90 per cent of Irish people look to the USA. Then they get romantic and bring in the fiddle.'

So, in the long run, just what exactly did The Virgin Prunes contribute to the development of modern Irish rock music? Although it is true that their global reputation has now reached almost mythic proportions, their devotees are small in number but intensely (irrationally?) unswerving. The Virgin Prunes were pure artists because they transcended audience expectations, taking them beyond a sphere of entertainment into something more primevally recognisable. The band were able to do this because they had the talent, the neck and the drive. The Virgin Prunes' principled, aesthetic output on both record and stage in the early 1980s has yet to be surpassed.

Gavin Friday: 'We kept Ireland safe for rock'n'roll? No... I think we and U2 inspired a lot of Irish punk bands. We proved that the guy up the road could play. We were younger than The Radiators From Space and The Boomtown Rats, and we had the working class credibility factor because we were from Ballymun. I think Gavin Friday gave men the confidence to dye their hair, put on some eyeliner and walk down Grafton Street. A few sublimi-

> '*Just about every Irish band that went to London never made it. Just think of it - every Irish band that went to London. Where are they now?*'
>
> KEVIN SHIELD,
> *My Bloody Valentine.*

nal things and influences are what The Virgin Prunes did, and it is in retrospect that they will be understood much better.'

Fragmented by the experience of splitting up, Gavin Friday now carries on as a successful, rather unique solo artist, as does Binttii – albeit somewhat less successfully. Guggi is now a respected artist, while the last remains of the band are now known simply as The Prunes, and are very much a straightforward, accomplished, guitar-oriented rock band.

It isn't that difficult to predict the future for avant-garde, rock-oriented music in Ireland. Since the mid-1980s demise of The Virgin Prunes as the sole perpetrators of art-shock rock, Ireland has had little involvement with or influence over the left-of-field fringe element. Groups such as My Bloody Valentine and The Whipping Boy started off in a flurry of guitar noise, the former travelling to London to authenticate their fulsome brand of white-noise pop, the latter to mutate into a relatively orthodox, albeit enjoyable guitar band.

The lines between the avant-garde and the commercial mainstream are getting less distinct as time goes by. What was considered outrageous and *outré* 10 years ago is now commonplace. The artists who consider themselves – or are considered by other people – to be unconventional are merely pretending to be something they're not.

The only person to inhabit what the average person or critic might call the

LEFT: *The Whipping Boy, keeping Ireland safe for white noise rock 'n'roll.*

other-worldly sphere of non-mainstream music is Aidan Walsh. Curiously enough, Gavin Friday became involved in the nascent career of Walsh, possibly seeing in him a kindred spirit and fellow time traveller. Walsh's perception of reality is not like that of others, which is not to say that his version of rock'n'roll isn't as valid as any orthodox rock band, merely that his employment and performance of it takes on different form and shape. What this means to the listener is anyone's guess…

Aidan Walsh first came to prominence in the mid-1980s, following his setting up of one of Dublin's first rehearsal studios. With the assistance of co-producers Gavin Friday and The Golden Horde's Simon Carmody, Walsh recorded his debut solo album, *A Life Story Of My Life* (1987), a collection of songs about aliens, food and the dispensing of free money! Despite the ramshackle atmosphere, the songs were just about held together by The Golden Horde's trashy backing. Either loved or loathed, the album's shock waves resounded through Dublin's rock élite. With his band, The Emperor's Eagles, Walsh produced a cacophonous high-pitched din and a charming sci-fi poetry mixed with a genuine theatre of the absurd. Career bands and serious rock pundits despised Walsh.

A strange Christmas

'Every man his prisoner, every woman his slave!' was the catchphrase from Walsh's second vinyl offering, the EP *Christmas In Four Dimension* (1988). A line-up of rock journalists and well-respected musicians accompanied Walsh, but the in-joke soon began to wear thin, and the self-proclaimed 'Emperor Of The Universe' was soon busily compiling a thick portfolio of his numerous press cuttings and planning a spectacular comeback that has yet to materialise.

Aside from Aidan Walsh, the only artists of nonconformist note are Gavin Friday, Pierce Turner, Antony and De Confidence, Binttii, and The Joshua Trio.

Gavin Friday pursued a post-Prunes dabble in painting before going back to the ideas he had germinated in the final days of the band. As has been evidenced, Friday looked towards Europe, in particular the 1920s/30s cabaret-as-comment style of presentation and singing. This framework was developed in The Blue Jaysus Cabaret, an impromptu series of off-kilter shows in Dublin's Waterfront Bar, that generated more hipness in several weeks than some bands manage in their entire careers.

Subsequently signing to Island records in the late 1980s, Friday delivered a handsome calling card with *Each Man Kills The Thing He Loves* (1990), the title taken from one of Friday's literary passions – Oscar Wilde's *The Ballad Of Reading Gaol*. Distinctly European flavoured, the album was received with knowing if somewhat muted praise. Far better accommodated was the follow-up album, *Adam'n'Eve* (1992), a collection of songs that saw Friday firmly entrenched in a cabaret style, but this time invested with a quick Dublin wit and a superb pop sensibility. 'This album could be the *Paradise Lost* of pop,' is Gavin Friday's cheeky résumé. Well he *would* say that, wouldn't he?

Before he joined up with The Virgin Prunes, Haa Lacka Binttii was plain old Danny Figgis. The Binttii *nom-de-Prune* was a Lypton Village tag. 'According to Gavin Friday,' recollects Binttii, 'the name meant humourless or lacking in ha-ha. He said it described my face which I took to be an insult of some kind.'

Figgis started his art rock career in 1978 as vocalist and keyboardist in a band called Normal Service Will Be Resumed As Soon As Possible, a punk-meets-Rick Wakeman conglomeration. On stage they had, according to Binttii: 'Dadaist cut-ups and ladies tied up in straitjackets. It was quite funny, but very pretentious.' He joined The Virgin Prunes at the beginning of 1980 and left in mid-1981. After a couple of years in apparent wilderness, he formed a band, Princess Tinymeat (so-called after Hollywood actor Montgomery Clift's reputedly small penis). Their debut single, 'Sloblands' (1985), caused an outcry due to the cover sleeve showing a naked Binttii. His other single releases, 'Bun In The Oven' (1986) and 'Devilcock' (1987) showcased their creator's sense of humour, wilful musical perversion and genuine talent. He's perceived by many in a variety of lights. Kieran Owens: 'He's a complete megalomaniac, self-believer and self-promoter, which is not a bad thing. His time hasn't come yet.'

Binttii: 'Some people think that I'm God's gift, witty, a wonderful person. And there are others who think I'm a noisy little faggot who makes a nuisance of himself. I'd leave out the faggot bit, but I am pretty obnoxious.' The world awaits an album release from Binttii with bated breath…

Pierce Turner's career has been documented elsewhere in this book, but suffice to say that his New York art-house experience has blended in with his Wexford background and produced music that relies heavily on the ambient, hypnotic textures of American minimalist composer Philip Glass. The best example of this *mélange* of styles can be found on Turner's debut album, ***It's Only A Long Way Across*** (1986). 'How It Shone' remains an exceptional piece of modern pop/avant-garde music. Turner has yet to better this and it's doubtful that he will, judging by his subsequent, more commercialised album releases.

Antony and De Confidence, on the other hand, have yet to break into the Irish collective consciousness, and it's equally doubtful that he/they will. Mainly a solo project, Cork's Antony has battled against both radio producers and music press for coverage to little avail. His idiosyncratic combination of electronics and poetry/rap have been interesting sidenotes in the development of Irish art-noise.

Which leaves The Joshua Trio…

The Joshua Trio were effectively born when U2's ***Rattle And Hum*** album was released in 1988. Previous to that (or at least from ***The Joshua Tree*** onwards) the idea of performing U2 songs in completely different musical styles had only been talked about. Free-form jazz renditions of 'Pride (In The Name Of Love)' were discussed, poems based on the more risible aspects of U2 – such as The Edge's bald spot, Bono's speeches, Adam Clayton's bass playing – were written. The result was a group that satirised what many people involved in Irish music regarded as the golden calf.

> *'The only people who I want to perceive me as heterosexual are women... The men can just bugger off, if you'll excuse the expression'*
>
> – BINTTII.

Initially looked upon by editors, executives and producers as a crude joke, The Joshua Trio finally got the last laugh when, in early 1992, they released a country & western version of 'The Fly', a song released on Son, a label directly connected to U2's very own Mother records!

Both through being-shortlisted on Britain's Radio One and beaming out from hip music programmes, The Joshua Trio have proved that by being funny as well as business smart, the non-mainstream way of doing things sometimes works even better than going through the normal channels. Their real concern is going to be one of follow-through: what can they do next? It should also be noted that the members of The Joshua Trio frequently moonlight as kitsch cabaret stars, Tony St. James and his Las Vegas Sound, a band who have managed to subvert Irish showband/cabaret shenanigans with often intentionally hilarious results.

Puzzling the punters

So where does that leave the purveyors of pop art and rock-shock? 'The problem,' says Kieran Owens, 'for all these avant-garde people – right back to the time of Tara Telephone and Mellow Candle – was that they were all extremely non-commercial enterprises, very much considering themselves as artists first and foremost. And if people didn't like it, then great; almost the ivory tower approach. There was a problem of appreciation for Joe Punter. You had the performers, the critics and the venues all supporting each other to justify

BELOW: *Pierce Turner blends an American pop ambience and Irish social attitude to create a Celtic soul synthesis.*

their own mutual existence. That made it difficult for the ordinary man in the street to say "That's a load of bollocks", because then the man in the street is told he's a pleb and is asked, "what do you know?"'

Kieran has a theory as to where the music will go. 'The intellectual reasons for a lot of this avant-garde stuff existing, which is primarily any form of music that in its day was considered dangerous – blues, jazz, rock'n'roll, punk – has gone out the window. Music now doesn't in any way form part of an expression of an intellectual resistance. As a generation of music lovers, we now find ourselves reliving the dreams, of an era long gone, of record company executives. Fourteen and 15-year-old kids don't have the slightest interest in music, they want to play Nintendo or Super Mario, or hack into computer data bases. Where the musical side of things is con-

> *'January 1: New Year's Resolution... I'm so quiet and shy I don't think I'll go out all this year.*
> *January 2: Complete change of mind!'*
>
> **Extract from the diaries of The Joshua Trio.**

cerned, people will have to consider what role there is going to be for a musician in this new entertainment pursuit.'

If that sounds too specifically non-parochial then Gavin Friday might just have a solution: 'Ireland has gone through a lot of changes in the last 10 years in a rock'n'roll context. Ten years ago, there was a degree of ambition and hunger, now everyone is sitting on their arses thinking they're brilliant, and the first sign of decay was with *The Commitments*, which is cancer to music development in Ireland. It's got nothing to do with Dublin. What 19-year-old in the early 1990s listens to "In The Midnight Hour"?'

'In Ireland, you have your U2 and your Hothouse Flowers fans or your tracksuit technos. As for what exactly is going to happen, I do not know. I am not going to go away...'

BELOW: *The Joshua Trio, irreverent, satirical and reportedly one of U2's favourite bands.*

PEAL

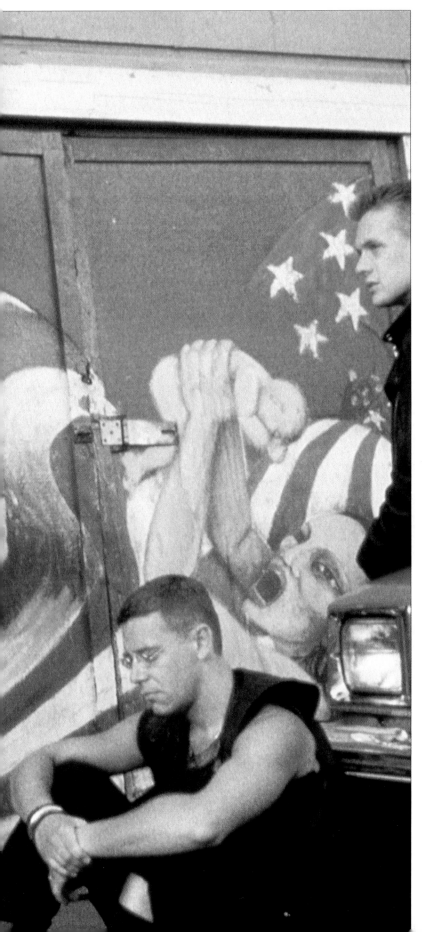

'I don't think I'd be able to write songs if I didn't have dreams. There wouldn't be much to write about or to look forward to.'

– LIAM O'MAONLAI OF
THE HOTHOUSE FLOWERS.

DOWN THROUGH THE YEARS IRISH acts have enjoyed more than their fair share of international success. In fact, in relation to the size of the country it has happened on quite a phenomenal scale.

The appeal has been based on a strong sense of national identity, both musically and personality-wise. While the more traditional-based acts like The Chieftains, De Danann and The Dubliners can lay claim to possessing an intrinsic Irish 'sound', Irish music now incorporates everything from rock to pop to rhythm'n'blues.

In the 1960s, Van Morrison and Rory Gallagher were the original leading lights, taking their unique, and, at times, visionary music, into Europe and the USA. As the 1970s rolled around, it was the turn of hard rockers (albeit imbued with a redeeming Celtic spirit) Thin Lizzy, to put the country on the map, with the band's leader Philip Lynott – a black Irishman – a true rock star of the old school.

That same decade also yielded Irish acts who were as diversely talented as balladeer Chris de Burgh, folk rockers Horslips and punk/pop outfit The Boomtown Rats. However, the success of all these artists could have prepared no one for the U2 phenomenon. They did for Ireland what pristine pop purveyors ABBA had previously done for Sweden, becoming one of the country's biggest exports. They highlighted their achievements even further by doggedly basing themselves at home.

LEFT: *U2 wanted to change the world, but settled for change within themselves.*

U2 utilised Irish studios, soundmen and recording engineers, and helped establish a strong infrastructure that has endured and expanded up to the present day. Subsequent bands have optimistically revelled in their inherent nativeness, with record companies, journalists and lawyers all enjoying the lucrative spin-off.

There was another reason for their staying at home – namely the Artists and Writers' Dispensation from Income Tax. In the case of an act the size of U2 (1987's *Joshua Tree* album has sold in excess of 14,000,000 copies to date), their tax-free income would be quite considerable.

U2's lead singer Bono has now changed his mind about Dublin as a starting base for fame and fortune, and advises struggling young Irish bands to journey to London where life is not quite so comfortable and safe. 'For years we've been encouraging Irish bands, telling them that they don't need to go abroad. But now I would never say to an Irish band "stay at home at all costs". There's maybe something too loose here (Dublin), too easy. You need to find a certain sharpness. You've got to go through the fire. If it is on your mind, I'd say go. Go to London and get burned.'

He believes that in the 1990s Dublin may be friendly, but it's not cool. 'Dublin is a warm place and that's the beauty of it. People here aren't afraid to make a fool of themselves. If anything links Dublin bands it's a lack of inhibition, we just don't conform to rock'n'roll's rigid form of cool. And you need that lack of inhibition to be creative. You've got to be prepared to jump off the deep end.'

Staying on home turf

Indeed the number of artists taking the emigrant trail had all but trickled out as the 1990s came in, with The Fat Lady Sings and Into Paradise two of the last bands to hop on the mail boat and seek fame and fortune in the bright lights of the big city called London.

While both experienced baptism by fire over the years, it is difficult to ascertain just how they would have fared had they based themselves at home. With nothing distinctly endemic about either of those outfits, they were left to succeed or fail on their own merits, without the patronage of either Irish press or pop stars.

In 1991, Into Paradise were dropped by their record label Ensign, but promptly returned to the pioneering Irish, but London-based, Setanta label who had actually issued the band's earlier recordings. Setanta is now a home from home for

BELOW: *Dave Long, lead singer of Into Paradise, looking skywards for some musical guidance.*

ABOVE: *Cathal Coughlan (left) and Sean O'Hagan of Microdisney in pensive pose.*

RIGHT: *The Fatima Mansions' primary excitable boy, Mr Cathal Coughlan.*

struggling young Irish bands and their acts also include The Divine Comedy and Brian.

Interestingly enough, Cork bands have always bypassed Dublin and headed straight to London to take their first tentative steps up the rock'n'roll ladder. Microdisney, who split into two bands – The Fatima Mansions and The High Llamas – are the most obvious example, though more recently, pop terrorists The Frank and Walters, and The Sultans Of Ping FC, have been burning rubber up and down Britain's motorways.

In Britain, the ex-Microdisney and current Fatima Mansions singer Cathal Coughlan has been hailed by music critics as one of the country's most interesting and important lyricists.

Yet London is no longer the gateway to the USA that it used to be; indeed in recent years the post-baggy, revivalist, dance-oriented British groups have certainly not been denting the American charts with anything approaching regularity.

In reality, U2 could have just as easily originated in Liverpool or Manchester as in Dublin. They drew on no Irish roots, although they did utilise the traditional skills of uilleann piper Vinny Kilduff (*October*, 1981) and fiddle player Steve Wickham (*War*, 1983).

The extra ingredient

Their sound was not dissimilar to some of their British contemporaries, such as Simple Minds and Echo and the Bunnymen, with its stark post-punk, guitar-based 'message'. Yet Bono and Co. were to be the 'chosen ones', with their quasi-evangelical sincerity undoubtedly assisting their passage.

Perhaps the highly religious background of three of the band members (the more fun-loving Adam Clayton did not subscribe to their Shalom Charismatic Christian movement) was something that could only have originated in Ireland.

This sincerity was to shine in early recordings such as 'Gloria', where Bono quoted heavily from a Latin prayer. U2 were the sort of rock'n'roll band your mother and father wouldn't mind coming round for afternoon tea. In their hands, guitars and drums were no longer subversive weapons, but rather a means to an end.

This simple message crossed all barriers and frontiers, from the suburban sprawl of Middle America to the slightly language-hampered inhabitants of the chilly North European mainland. A white flag allowed instant communication.

LEFT: *Bono: from LA to Galway, from Berlin to Memphis, always searching for his musical roots.*

Years later, U2 were to take part in a tribute to folk masters The Dubliners on RTE's *Late Late Show*, with Bono speaking fondly of the late Luke Kelly of the band. Trying to find any Luke Kelly or Dubliners influences in U2's music would indeed be a thankless and time-consuming task. However, Bono later revealed that his latter-day fascination with Irish music and the ballad form was due to a certain confusion which was surrounding his band's identity (or lack of same), and the appeal of the sheer humanity and common past of which the form is an inherent part.

On 1990's ambitious *Bringing It All Back Home* TV series, which theorised on Irish music journeying to the USA and being exported back years later, he sang a new original, Irish-influenced tune called 'My Wild Irish Rose' (reportedly the ballad was finished literally minutes before the cameras arrived).

It was another typical move by a band frantically searching for musical roots throughout the world. From Memphis to Galway, from Berlin to Los Angeles, they explored every culture with the fervent zeal of musical missionaries. Astonishingly, their fans stuck with them as the musical magpies explored new avenues. It is something that continues to astound the band.

> 'We've started to make records now for ourselves and for our own audience who do listen very carefully to all our records and who do spot all the subtleties. We're The Grateful Dead of the 1990s'
>
> BONO of U2.

Bono again: 'They (the fans) are one step ahead of us in some ways. Rather than to have to lead the audience around by the nose we get the sense that they are right behind us every step of the way. We thought that if we stripped away the U2 sound completely, if we immersed ourselves in gospel music, country, soul... we're bound to shake off at least 50 per cent of U2 fans: they can't cope with this. But they really could. As long as the songs are good then they will go with us all the way. When we start writing shit songs then I will know that it is over.'

Indeed sometimes it seems that the music U2 produce is secondary to their appeal as icons. Sincerity, image and the feeling of being part of a mass movement are the key components as far as the fans are concerned. U2's message is a simple one of peace, love and understanding, a cry to dispossessed souls everywhere to come together at Bono's bidding.

However in recent years the band have deliberately deflated their once-pompous image, and a distinct sense of irony and humour now permeates their public appearances. Their songs have also noticeably improved, and they have become far more focussed and personalised.

RIGHT: *Sinead O'Connor, controversial and complex. She remains one of Ireland's most successful female recording artists.*

While a single such as 'The Fly' (1991) can still shoot to the top of the British charts, there were shouts of 'foul play' at the time of its release. This revolved around the fact that it was a limited edition, with fans rushing to buy copies before they disappeared. A shrewd marketing ploy, pure coincidence or an enigmatic exercise? Who knows, but one can't really blame a band in that position for not taking any chances after a lengthy lay-off.

There is a distinct Irish sound, but it is difficult to pinpoint the forces that come together to create it. In the 1980s, Irish music certainly began to come into its own, with Sinead O'Connor, Enya, Christy Moore, Chris de Burgh, Clannad, Paul Brady and The Hothouse Flowers all experiencing the warm glow of worldwide appeal and acclaim.

Meanwhile the great Van Morrison steadfastly toiled away, bringing his famed 'Caledonian soul' around the world to a highly dedicated following, all waiting to lap up the next regular instalment of his mystical, soul-searching Celtic roots music.

Upon analysis, it is apparent that each Irish artist had a strong sense of identity about them. Sinead O'Connor can release a Prince song, but then she's just as likely to record a traditional unaccompanied Irish tune. A complex and complicated character, she shifts quickly between being perceived as a Bambi in bovver boots, a tear-stained waif, and a tough, independent young mother who is not afraid to speak her mind.

Her outspokenness on everything from her objections to American venues playing the 'Star Spangled Banner' before her concerts and censorship in rock music, to her once abrasive views on U2 and the IRA, and Ireland's peculiar political stance on abortion and divorce have all frequently landed her in boiling water.

Frank Sinatra may have wanted to 'kick her ass' and rap man Hammer may have offered her a one-way ticket from the USA (she based herself briefly in Los Angeles) back to Ireland, but along with Enya she is the biggest female singing star to come out of Ireland since, well, Dana (who won the Eurovision Song Contest in 1970 with 'All Kinds Of Everything'. The song was later adapted by U2 parodyists The Joshua Trio,

who changed the chorus line to 'All kinds of everything remind me of U2').

O'Connor has railed (quite rightly) against the false and destructive materialistic values of the music industry, but to take the argument to its logical conclusion would necessitate her abandoning her career entirely – something of a drastic solution.

Again, as with U2, her fans care not one whit for her frequent U-turns, emotive outbursts and general 'rent-a-quote' activities. Her records and performances remain the bottom line, although a little bit of controversy never did anybody any harm and her self-contradictions are rapidly swept aside.

O'Connor was never again to return to live in Ireland after her initial move to London during the mid-1980s. Over the years, she has consistently castigated Dublin, but her native country has greatly inspired her.

She was emotionally shaped and moulded by her background, before coming to the attention of Ensign records after spells with Dublin bands In Tua Nua and Ton Ton Macoute.

Her rise to the top was inevitable and inexorable, and her emotionally stark and painful music looks set to endure. She is without doubt one of the most intriguing artists that Ireland has ever produced.

Outspoken Irish acts shouting their way to the top are nothing new, motormouth Bob Geldof having paved the way several years before for Ms O'Connor. The Boomtown Rats were one of the finest chart bands of the 1970s, seemingly effortlessly narrowing the once-yawning chasm between local acclaim and international success.

When Geldof spat out his frustration at standing in a dole queue in the rain ('Looking After Number One', 1977), listeners outside his native country were able to relate to his sense of desperation, urgency and sheer frustration.

However, The Boomtown Rats were never to conquer the USA, the story going that Geldof insulted the all-powerful bigwigs of the American music industry when they came to watch the band perform at a special showcase gig.

The Rats wholeheartedly embraced rhythm and blues, fusing it with their own innate pop sensibility. The formula was to

> '*The reason I cut it sounds really boring but there was this geezer in London who I really fancied and who had the same hairstyle. So I thought if I cut my hair off I might might have a chance. It didn't work, but I liked the haircut so much I kept it*'
>
> SINEAD O'CONNOR.

RIGHT: The calm visage of Sinead O'Connor hides an inward sense of outrage towards all types of social and sexual hypocrisy.

RIGHT: *Lights, action and sound at Live Aid. Organiser Bob Geldof raises his fist in defiance of Third World poverty and starvation.*

endure for several years, before the inspiration which had driven the band eventually dried up, and the hits stopped coming.

Even the post-Live Aid/Band Aid image of the saintly Sir Bob, who seemingly had every world leader's private line in his address book, could not resuscitate their flagging career. Geldof may have been the world's best known Irishman during the mid-1980s, but The Rats simply couldn't get hit records.

They disbanded in 1986, with Geldof's subsequent solo career experiencing varying peaks and troughs. For **The Vegetarians Of Love** (1990) he embraced his Celtic roots (hitherto well-disguised), delving into the celebrated songwriting styles of the prolific Van Morrison and the late Phil Lynott for inspiration. It worked, and Geldof's next move will be watched with interest.

Bold Irish pop singers have not cornered the market entirely, with quality and perseverance also winning out. Donegal-born singer Enya's New Age, hot tub music has translated remarkably well around the world. From the Far East to the shores of

Tripoli to the LA Freeway, her ethereal and slightly spacey songs have touched a common chord in the CD generation.

She receives a steady volume of fan mail from all around the world. The people who feel the need to communicate with her believe that her haunting songs have somehow become intertwined with their lives, helping them over difficult, trauma-fraught periods like the death of a loved one or the breakup of a marriage.

A shy performer

Enya is very comfortable with the level of success she has achieved to date and is extremely wary of progressing to a higher level of fame for fear of too much pressure. 'I'd have difficulty with that because I'm a very shy, private person,' she says. While some deride her inherently traditional-based music as being of an overtly depressing nature, her strong melodies certainly have a soothing charm.

Varying emotions, from anger to happiness to sadness, are utilised in creating her carefully textured recordings. These can

take many years to create, as she toils away in the home studio she owns with partners Nicky and Roma Ryan. Roma writes the lyrics for all the tunes, while her husband Nicky engineers and produces the sessions. Both manage Enya's career. The unassuming, soft-spoken singer has her own way of dealing with success, and is not sure if it will be important to her for the rest of her life.

Enya: 'It's difficult to come back down from success, but working in the studio mellows me out. You get concerned about the music and the scale of success is lowered tremendously. You're also out of the limelight. And when you come back the scale of success is right back down again.'

Enya comes from a veritable musical dynasty, and actually began her career as a member of Clannad, alongside her older sister Maire Brennan, brothers Paul and Ciaran, and uncles Padraig and Noel Duggan. But it was to be a brief liaison, and she soon departed the ranks to forge a solo career, with Clannad soundman Nicky Ryan accompanying her.

The Gweedore, Donegal, family have been making music since the early 1970s (their father Leo having played in local dance bands), for many years singing in their native Gaelic tongue. Their heavenly vocal harmonies are backed by harp, flute, acoustic guitars, keyboards and double bass, creating a highly distinctive and immediately recognisable wall of sound.

As Irish as a certain black brew they have been known to promote in TV advertisements, Clannad's music reeks of open turf fires, Donegal heather and an age-old tradition.

Just when it looked like they could go no further in their chosen field, they surprised everybody by clocking up a Top 10 hit in 1982 with their 'Theme From Harry's Game'. It was taken from a highly successful TV series about an undercover agent operating in Northern Ireland and flawlessly fused modern technology with wispy, delicate vocal harmonies.

Further success was just around the corner when they were commissioned to provide the haunting music for the TV show *Robin Of Sherwood*. This yielded the 1984 hit album **Legend**. The Clannad sound is now readily identifiable worldwide.

Two years later, U2's Bono was to team up with them to perform a duet with Maire on the song 'In A Lifetime', which became,

> **'Interviews are sometimes like going to a psychiatrist'**
>
> ENYA.

BELOW: *Enya found international success for her dreamy melodies and astute encapsulation of an Irish sensibility.*

naturally enough, a hit. By then, Clannad had become a truly international act.

Since then, despite the occasional line-up adjustment, they have consolidated their position, while experimenting from time to time with other musical forms. But they have always returned to their own distinct style. It's a success story that will last for exactly as long as they wish.

In a totally different ballpark is romantic pop balladeer Chris de Burgh. The Dublin-based songwriter (for whom it is nearly always Saint Valentine's Day) admits that beneath his refined and cultured tones there lurks a man of steel. He believes strongly that a certain tenacity is vital to survive in the murky, shark-infested waters of the international music business.

'You have to be incredibly tough,' he states emphatically. 'I never give anybody that impression, but I can tell you that I am. I'm steel inside, because I have been dropped so many times.'

However, de Burgh is philosophical about success. 'Chart positions are not like the Olympics,' he believes. 'It's not the best person in the world who wins, just whoever happens to be there at the time. I reckon I could have had a Number 1 record with my song "Missing You" if it hadn't been for the Coca Cola song that was out at the time. I think that it's unfair to have a song that's running as an advert as well.'

> *'If I'm in New York or in Cork I don't need to meet up with loads of people afterwards and rave the night away. I just finish my gig and I split. I go to bed, get up early the next morning and go for a walk'*
>
> CHRISTY MOORE.

While de Burgh is enormously popular in Ireland, Britain and the rest of Europe, his appeal has not yet translated to the USA. It's not something that unduly upsets him. 'My prime concern was always Europe, I have never been that interested in America. It's a difficult place to tour and in many cases very ugly. I think the satisfaction you'd get in breaking into America is if you're interested in money. It's like robbing the bank, or breaking the bank. But that's never been my motivation.'

Yet his songs for not-so-swinging lovers are incredibly successful and de Burgh must be acknowledged as something of a master craftsman with a winning formula.

Christy Moore is another Irish solo performer whose homespun appeal has translated abroad. While de Burgh sings of women in red, strippers called Patricia and ferrymen who must under no circumstances be paid, Moore is a man with a mission to tell it as he sees it. Yet he denies that he is a crusader looking for causes.

The man they call the 'Storm in a T-shirt' moved to England in the mid-1960s and began playing guitar and singing in pubs, supplementing his income by working on building sites, oil rigs and as a cold meats porter.

The lone star

Still operating in the folk idiom, the former member of both Planxty and Moving Hearts now packs out concert halls around the world, armed only with his acoustic guitar, his bodhran (a portable goat-skinned percussive instrument), his razor-sharp wit and downhome honesty.

Moore: 'I'm not saying that what I have is magical, but this communication between an audience and a performer is some intangible thing. I don't know where it comes from or what it is. But you can feel it when you've connected, it's a magical thing.'

In 1991, Christy left WEA and set up his own Newberry record label with manager Mattie Fox. Moore explains: 'If I was in London or New York and they had a new Madonna or Prince record coming out they (the record company) didn't give a shit

RIGHT: *Chris de Burgh, romantic, balladic and sentimental troubador, is the people's choice as a songwriter supreme.*

about me. They might put up a poster in the office stating "Atlantic welcomes Christy Moore to New York", but as soon as you're gone they take it down, y'know?'

He frequently experiences homesickness in the course of his extensive travels. 'In Australia I got that feeling, but I think it was the sheer geographical separation from family, home and country. In a strange way I have this feeling that I know everybody in Ireland. I can't explain it, but it's genuinely the way I feel sometimes.'

Indeed Moore has now achieved legendary status at home. Instead of endlessly touring the country he now books into a spacious and strategic Dublin venue for a couple of weeks and fans come from far and near to see and hear him.

His songs are pertinent and often touching. He has sung about the Birmingham Six, the illegal immigrants in the USA and the stark hypocrisies and injustices in Irish society. Moore offers no rose-tinted view of modern Ireland, and his concert performances run the gamut from hilarious commentary to thought-provoking messages on social and political issues.

Paul Brady's muse has led him down several different paths over the years. Born in Strabane, Northern Ireland, on May 6 1947, he was initially an active participant in the Dublin beat group boom of the 1960s. Brady subsequently entered the folk and traditional Irish areas as a member of The Johnstons and Planxty, later becoming one half of a duo with fellow ex-Planxty man Andy Irvine.

Just when it looked like he was going to carve out a lifelong career for himself as a successful cult folk figure, Brady decided to return to his electric roots. The result was **Hard Station** (1981), which stands today as his finest work in the rock idiom. Several other albums followed, but perfection frequently overtook inspiration, with the result that most were criminally over-produced, and lacked the immediacy and spontaneity of **Hard Station**.

A tough taskmaster

A passionate and intense performer, Paul Brady demands the listener's complete involvement when he's working in a rock framework, something that has possibly mitigated against his own success.

Curiously enough it was as a songwriter instead of as a performer that Brady was to win true international acclaim. To date, Tina Turner, Dave Edmunds, Santana and Bonnie Raitt have all covered his songs. He has also been favourably namechecked by no less a personage than the great bard

ABOVE: *Christy Moore: his live performances cover the spectrum from satirical comment to serious social and political messages.*

RIGHT: *Paul Brady captures the romantic essence of both folk and rock.*

himself, Bob Dylan. While Brady's standing as a performer and a recording artist is guaranteed, it is as a songwriter that he will undoubtedly reap his just rewards, both financial and otherwise.

The Hothouse Flowers are part of a younger generation of music makers. Formed by native Irish speakers Liam O'Maonlai and Fiachna O'Braonain, their unique sound is steeped in an Irish musical heritage, with the highly enigmatic O'Maonlai claiming a debt to the old 'Sean-Nos' (unaccompanied songs sung in the Irish language) singers. When they are not involved in rock'n'roll, the pair can often be found participating in traditional sessions in small pubs for the sheer fun of it.

'We just have it (the Irish language) and we don't hide it,' explains O'Maonlai. 'It has been very good to us. Before anybody else in RTE (the Irish radio and TV station) was interested in us, the bulk of our interviews and appearances were on Irish language programmes.'

Hothouse Flowers have married a subtle traditional influence with rock, soul and blues, a heady combination that has resulted in successful world tours as far afield as Australia and the USA. Their single 'Don't Go' rode up the British charts on the back

LEFT: *Hothouse Flowers are a successful hybrid of Irish traditional influences, rock, soul and blues.*

of a guest spot on the 1988 Eurovision Song Contest, but they failed to capitalise on its success, and another British Top 10 hit was not forthcoming.

In fact it wasn't until the release of their second album, *Home* (1990), that they revealed they were not one-hit-wonders, and were actually capable of penning more decent tunes. It was, in patches, a highly evocative album, as O'Maonlai joyfully sang of the bells of Dublin's Christchurch Cathedral ('Christchurch Bells') ringing out across the city.

Using a wide variety of producers, including illustrious names such as Alan Winstanley, Daniel Lanois and Clive Langer, it showed that the band were coming to terms with both their musical roots and their songwriting abilities. The best is probably yet to come in the case of The Hothouse Flowers.

In Britain, second and even third generation Irish have frequently reverted to their homeland for insipiration, the two most notable examples being The Pogues and Elvis Costello.

The Pogues dragged Irish music through a hedge backwards, in the process fusing it with the dual delights of punk and drinking sessions. It was music that transcended all barriers and creeds, and offended the pre-cious sensibilities of the purists, who would rather see the music locked away in a sugar-strewn glass cage and carefully taken out for examination on Sundays and Holy Days of Obligation.

Led by Shane MacGowan, who was born in London of Tipperary parents, The Pogues blazed a trail of hazardous glory for the best part of a decade before the increasingly sozzled MacGowan was 'invited to leave' the line-up. The Pogues' story to date has been thoroughly documented, and whether the band will be able to survive without MacGowan's songwriting skills, and him without their support and musicianship, remains to be seen. Whatever happens to be the outcome, through MacGowan's tunes and the band's liaisons with the likes of The Dubliners, they certainly turned Irish music on its head and brought it to a worldwide audience.

Born in Merseyside, Elvis Costello's Irish ancestors had settled there some three generations before. Costello now owns a house outside Dublin, where he and his wife Cait O'Riordan (formerly bassist with The Pogues) spend much of their free time.

Some of his latter-day recordings have utilised traditional Irish instruments, and Costello (real name Declan MacManus)

> *'My dad told me I was a dreamer years ago. And a clown, and a yo-yo, and a clot'*
>
> LIAM O'MAONLAI of *The Hothouse Flowers.*

RIGHT: *Elvis Costello flits from style to style with no apparent discomfort. He has used orchestral strings, traditional Irish music and full-blown rock to fulfil his vision of what music should be.*

even turned up to compose and sing a number on The Chieftains' 1991 Christmas album *The Bells Of Dublin*.

Costello also participated in the *Bringing It All Back Home* TV series, singing an original number called 'Mischievous Ghost'. It also featured the vocal talents of the flame-haired Irish chanteuse Mary Coughlan and the former Moving Hearts uilleann piper Davy Spillane.

The former bug-eyed monster who appeared to come from the planet Revenge, and who has long since left the so-called new wave behind, compares his current liking of Irish music with something as basic as his fondness for sunshine.

While traditionally-rooted Irish bands such as The Chieftains (arguably the coun-

try's premier musical ambassadors), De Danann and Stockton's Wing have exported their sound all around the world down through the years, in the mid-1980s Scotsman Mike Scott generously decided to give Irish music back to the Irish.

He formed a new raggle taggle version of his Waterboys group and moved to Spiddal, County Galway, where he recorded two albums that reflected his obsession with the genre. *Fisherman's Blues* (1988) was an erratic mixture of rock, Irish and country influences, with local 'character' Tomas McKeown reciting the WB Yeats poem 'The Stolen Child'.

The following album, *Room To Roam* (1990), was diddley aye heaven or hell, depending on your viewpoint. After several

ABOVE: *Trad band The Chieftains are living proof that age does not diminish the creative spirit.*

brief forays abroad with the traditional line-up (featuring an array of flutes, accordian and fiddles) that recorded both albums, Scott broke the band up in 1991. When last heard of, he had returned to his rock roots and moved to New York.

Irish music can no longer be easily classified as uilleann pipes, fiddles and turf fires. A whole world of possibilities has been opened up, with U2, Sinead O'Connor, Mary Black, Mary Coughlan and the Hothouse Flowers now as identifiably Irish as The Chieftains or The Dubliners.

The music is not a beast that can be easily traced or tamed. Demarcation lines have now been crossed so many times that the signs have become blurred. From the Dockers pub on Dublin's quays to Doolin in County Clare pilgrimages are made to seek its essence.

RIGHT: *Along with Sinead O'Connor, Mary Coughlan is another fiery female Irish vocalist.*

κ BANDS

A FTER THE EUPHORIA AND EXCITE-MENT that greeted the arrival of *The Commitments* movie, many people were predicting that Dublin would turn into a new soul capital. This has yet to happen (it's unlikely that it ever will), and very few bands have opted to follow the path of the celebrated 'twelve disciples of soul'.

American soul music has not been, and never will be, endemic to Ireland but, as the buzz about the movie fades, many of the musicians involved are furiously pushing their own projects. Consequently, there are now more bands than ever in existence, and although many never make it out of the rehearsal rooms or garages, it has resulted in Dublin becoming labelled as the 'City Of 1,000 Rock Bands'.

From the Baggot Inn and The Attic to Bad Bobs and the Rock Garden, bands are busy plying their wares and dreaming of rock'n'roll stardom. Walk through the trendy Temple Bar 'Left Bank' area of the city any evening and a musical cacophony fills the air. Electronic dreams ring loudly around the cobblestones as bands rehearse or record in the myriad of adjacent studios. The pubs are later filled with band members who will discuss the latest rumours, while informing anybody who is willing to listen of their own plans.

Simon Carmody's band The Golden Horde have been together since 1984, and in 1991 released their eponymous debut album on U2's Mother label. 'Being in a band now is considered a career apprentice-ship', says Carmody over a cider in the Dockers pub on Dublin's south quays. 'But I think that rock'n'roll should be a disgrace, it definitely shouldn't be about reinforcing the bland centre of society.'

LEFT: *The Golden Horde are determined to live out the reality of rock'n'roll fantasy.*

The singer claims that his band represents freedom and truth, 'the electronic sound of freedom', as he so eloquently puts it. The great bohemian/rebel tradition of Ireland is an influence and inspiration to artists and performers, as well as the fact that bands no longer have to leave the country to make it. Nor have the colourful cartoon rockers, who try to combine the finest elements of The Ramones, Phil Spector, The Sweet and The Beach Boys in their very own sonic assault, been compromised by signing on the dotted line with Mother. Prior to that they financed their own releases, including two mini-albums.

'Rock'n'roll isn't worth doing if it's compromised', Carmody snorts in disgust. 'We're certainly not careerists, but we do want to put rock'n'roll back into the mainstream. We're about a headfuck thing... an explosion. And you get burned out if you light a fire every time.'

The mainstream is where most of the current crop of Irish bands long to be as they play cat and mouse games with the international record companies. The leather jacket has been replaced by the three-piece suit in the game of rebellion, as they seek to claw their way to the top.

While there may be 1,000 bands out there, many industry insiders believe that there certainly are not 1,000 good or even

> *'All I live for is the kids at the front, singing and dancing'*
>
> SIMON CARMODY
> of The Golden Horde.

competent managers, vital components in any band's career. A non-musical friend of the band who has access to a car and a telephone will no longer suffice, as the high-powered negotiations are entered into with bean counters, lawyers and other music business hit men.

Beefy singer Andrew Strong, who played the monstrous lead singer 'Deco Cuffe' in *The Commitments*, signed to MCA Records in 1991 in the slipstream of ecstasy that followed the movie's release. The bull-necked belter, who favours the occasional Joe Cocker-style painful grimace when reaching for the high notes, soon found himself in the USA, songwriting with soul legend Lamont Dozier and sharing a stage with Wilson Pickett.

Strong subsequently formed his own backing band and went out on the road to cater for soul-starved Commitments fans. Whether he can become a truly original artist instead of a cabaret-style interpreter of old soul classics remains to be seen.

He began singing at the age of 11, learning the ropes from his father Rob, a veteran Irish performer in the rock/soul/funk vein. As a firsthand observer of his father's career, Andrew soon learned that talent and perseverance alone did not always bring financial reward and critical acclaim. His own fame has resulted in a spin-off success

LEFT: *Before* The Commitments, *the singer Andrew Strong was completely unknown. Now, he is one of Ireland's best-known musical exports.*

for his father, and in March 1992 Rob Strong signed a recording deal with Polygram Records in Ireland.

'I have to do my own thing', smiles Andrew on the subject of his jet-setting lifestyle which keeps him away from home and family for much of the year. Strong has also turned into a highly unlikely sex symbol of sorts, and has been mobbed everywhere from the expansive Square shopping centre in the suburban sprawl that is Dublin's Tallaght, to the famous Tower Records in Los Angeles.

'I even tried wearing a disguise,' he says, 'but it didn't work'. Fame does have its compensations, and Strong is now in the rather enviable position of being able to afford a house in both Los Angeles and in his own beloved Wicklow.

His mother Noreen, who managed several bands in Ireland, looked after Andrew's affairs until what they considered the right manager came along. After offers from the managers of Madonna, Lenny Kravitz and Janet Jackson, they settled on Ged Doherty, who had proved his mettle guiding the careers of English singers Alison Moyet and

Paul Young. Doherty sees a hard road ahead for the young Irishman with the iron lungs, but the triple-platinum sales of the first Commitments album will undoubtedly help. With the release of the second album from the movie and Andrew's own solo album, he will have had every shot at the big time that a young singer could hope for.

Another 'Commitment' to secure a recording deal is Robert Arkins, who played streetwise manager 'Jimmy Rabbitte' in the movie. Arkins, who was fronting his own band called Housebroken before the celluloid career opportunity that he couldn't turn down came knocking on his door, is also signed to MCA as a solo artist. He is unsure about whether the album will be sold as a joint effort or as a solo project.

Arkins and his band play music of the anachronistic 1970s jazz/funk variety, where musicians are given their heads and audiences are near-intruders on seemingly interminably long jam sessions. It is highly doubtful if it will ever break through to a wider pop/rock audience.

He is also anxious to play down his 'Commitments' connection; it will certainly not assist his passage to fame. 'I'm not in a rush to jump on *The Commitments* band-wagon like Andrew Strong. Also, I don't want people to get confused and think of me as an actor instead of as a musician', explains the laid-back young singer who also plays the trumpet and bass guitar.

Arkins goes on to state, quite paradoxically it would appear, that he would love to do more acting work, but MCA want him to concentrate on his music career.

Other Commitments who are making active career moves with their respective bands include Glen Hansard (The Frames), Dick Massey (The Sindicate), Maria Doyle-Kennedy (Black Velvet Band), Dave Finnegan (The Brood) and Ken McCluskey (D11 Runners). Only The Frames and The Black Velvet Band have obtained international record deals, which they signed before the movie. The other bands are slowly discovering that a connection with Alan Parker and a hit movie does not automatically guarantee a lucrative international recording career.

Ultimately, we will have to wait several years to gauge the effect that *The Commitments* cottage industry will have made on the Irish music scene. Only a cou-

> **'It (The Commitments) *was great crack, a lot more fun making it than talking about it in fact'***
>
> *'COMMITMENTETTE' MARIA DOYLE-KENNEDY of The Black Velvet Band.*

ple of the participants look set for stardom (and even then that's not guaranteed), and it could result in the detrimental effect that U2's success had in the 1980s, where every mother's son felt that he too could forge a career in music just by picking up a battered guitar and knocking out a few tunes. Whatever happens, post-Commitments Dublin is still abuzz with activity, as young performers realise that dreams can occasionally come true. Holding on to them is the problem.

The now notoriously irreverent Saw Doctors, who hail from Galway, are one of the most successful of all Irish bands to have achieved fame in recent years, and they have occasionally surpassed the studio-sequestered U2 and The Hothouse Flowers. Their single 'I Useta Love Her' (1990) soon became something of a second National Anthem, and was heard in every place that people gathered to drink and make merry.

They managed to strike something of a common chord with the entire Irish nation, with everybody from grey-haired talk show hosts to trendy priests commenting on how the terribly cheeky chappies rhymed 'Sunday mass' with 'the glory of her ass' in 'I Useta Love Her'.

BELOW: *Lead singer with The Frames and former Commitment, Glen Hansard, is keen to differentiate between his past and present musical preoccupations.*

They have appeared on Irish TV in a variety of side-splitting guises, from Gardai (Irish policemen) to overgrown altar boys and soldiers. The Doctors, who hail from the small country town of Tuam in County Galway, give not a toss for fashion, trends or style, and their basic tenet seems to be to have as much of a hoot as possible in the time available to them. This can occasionally obscure their inherent gift for conjuring up a strong melody and a spot of accurate social commentary.

Knockout gigs

Unquestionably, 1991 was their year. They effortlessly stole the Feile three-day festival in Thurles from under the noses of some of the more serious 'artistes', they successfully ran a major concert in the football stadium of their own home town during the late autumn, and they rang in the New Year by headlining their own concert in Dublin's prestigious Point Theatre. The only previous acts to have played such seasonal concerts in the venue have been U2 and The Hothouse Flowers.

Some jaundiced observers feel that The Saw Doctors have put Irish rock music back by the best part of a decade with their 'designer culchie' (a 'culchie' being anybody from outside Dublin) stance. Still, any band that can upset so many po-faced rock critics must be doing something right!

'We'd prefer to be daft than boring,' comments The Saw Doctors' guitarist Leo Moran, with regard to the subject of the band's high jinks. 'Yes, we do take ourselves seriously to a degree, but as long as it's in tune and powerful, we don't mind.'

He believes that people enjoy the mirror image of most of their songs, many of which are based on real life characters from, and events in, Tuam. They did not begin the band with a long term career in mind, though it has certainly turned into something like that now.

According to Leo, having a Number 1 Irish single for eight weeks was 'stone daft...it just doesn't make any sense.'

The Saw Doctors are probably too parochial to translate significantly outside Ireland, except of course wherever young rural emigrants have gathered, which is just about everywhere from the USA to Australia. In 1991, their first tentative steps into the USA were well-received, although Leo revealed that the band were seriously hampered by none of their records being available there at the time.

They have also toured Britain with The Waterboys, after Mister Raggle Taggle himself, Mike Scott, took them under his wing for a spell. He even produced their debut single 'N 17' and appeared on stage at Feile '91 with the band, singing a song that they all had just composed the day before.

With their broad smiles, friends in high places, irreverent attitudes and catchy ditties, The Saw Doctors will be around for some time to come.

The current wave of acts hoping to break through includes, deep breath, An Emotional Fish, The Forget Me Nots, The Pale, Something Happens, Power Of Dreams, Black Velvet Band, The Fat Lady Sings, The 4 Of Us, The Sultans Of Ping FC, The Joshua Trio, Andy White, Blink, Therapy?, The Blue Angels, A House, My Little Funhouse and The Cranberries.

RIGHT: *Dublin band Power of Dreams have the experience and idealism of youth on their side.*

Also signed to the successful independent Irish label Solid, who inked a major worldwide distribution deal with Warners in 1992, are Galway bands The Stunning and Toasted Heretic, as well as Dublin noise boys Whipping Boy and tough leather-jacketed rockers The Honey Thieves.

U2's Mother label also changed its approach as the 1990s rolled in, deciding to develop bands on a more long-term basis instead of on the previous one-off single releases (In Tua Nua, Cactus World News etc). Acts currently on their roster that are making interesting noises include Engine Alley and The Golden Horde, while the sister label Son has Christie Hennessy, a talented songwriter who at 40-something must be somewhat amused at winning several Best Newcomer awards in 1991/2!

Indeed, there seems to be a new wave of irreverence coupled with an emphasis on good old-fashioned entertainment developing. From The Sultans Of Ping FC and The Pale, to The Golden Horde, The Joshua Trio and The Frank And Walters, the bottom line is definitely fun and frolics.

> *'No I'm not sensible at all. I haven't got a head on me shoulders'*
>
> NIALL O'FLAHERTY
> *of The Sultans Of Ping FC.*

BELOW: *A House have the knack of writing superbly commercial songs with a subversive subtext.*

RIGHT: *Galway band Toasted Heretic have been widely acclaimed for their eccentric but identifiable pop music.*

From Cork city, The Sultans Of Ping FC stormed the British charts in 1992 (reaching the dizzy heights of 60-something) with their dazzling debut single 'Where's Me Jumper?'. The band had been spotted the previous year at the annual Cork Rocks showcase gigs by Martin Heath, the head of trendy British dance label Rhythm King. He decided that he must have them. They thought that he was joking, as no record company had ever expressed the remotest interest in their music. Contracts were duly produced and signed, and the wacky four-piece soon embarked on a lengthy British tour to back up the release of their record.

The band are obsessed with football ('Give Him A Ball And A Yard Of Grass'), girls ('Veronica'), misplaced mohair jumpers ('Where's Me Jumper?') and exotic non-alcoholic cocktails ('Two Pints Of Raza'). A Sultans of Ping performance involves much audience participation, with fans frequently lying on their backs to indulge in a spot of 'air cycling'. They may not be the future of rock'n'roll as we know it, but they sure ain't boring!

Dublin three-piece The Pale signed to A&M Records late in 1991. With a curious line-up of vocals, bass, mandolin and drum machine, their sound has something of a mid-European feel to it, and has been described by some as casbah meets ceilidh.

Fronted by Matthew Devereux, who could feasibly be the second most famous bald person to come out of Ireland since Sinead O'Connor (the band are managed by Columb Farrelly, who was previously a member of an old O'Connor band, Ton Ton Macoute), they sing songs about subjects as diverse as willies and dogs with no tails. The band are fans of The Brothers Grimm, and describe their songs as nursery rhymes.

While there is a novelty value to their act, they are talented enough as songwriters and musicians to endure well beyond the dreaded initial Flavour Of The Month phase.

The Joshua Trio (they're actually a four-piece) have wholeheartedly dedicated themselves to spreading the word of Bono and his buddies around the world. After an enforced lay-off of nearly two years while U2 were in Berlin and other locations creating their *Achtung Baby* offering, the Trio re-emerged during November 1991, and they haven't looked back since.

> '*It's not necessary for everybody to have major success and be a huge platinum-selling act. All that's necessary for yourself is that you actually enjoy what you're doing and feel that you're getting somewhere*'
>
> NICK KELLY *of The Fat Lady Sings.*

Their fetchingly berobed leader Paul Wonderful has been known to arrive at the Baggot Inn on a donkey, while the band now carry a large stained glass window, featuring Bono instead of the standard religious icons, as part of their backdrop. Wonderful is always 'in character', as he drawls away in Bono's best post-*Rattle And Hum* mid-American accent.

So are The Joshua Trio genuine irreverent tricksters or merely court jesters wheeled out at regular intervals to entertain and massage the egos of Ireland's royal family of rock? Make up your own mind, but hurry, because the joke certainly won't last forever.

Like The Sultans Of Ping FC, The Frank And Walters hail from Cork city in the South of Ireland. The three-piece outfit with a penchant for stirring Beatle-type melodies and a spot of eccentricity, took their name from two oddball characters who lived near them. 'They were a bit mad', explains their bass player Paul Linehan. 'Actually I'm not even sure if they're still alive. They moved to England when we were around twelve years old and we haven't seen them since.'

The Franks in turn moved to London in the autumn of 1991, basing themselves in the decidedly non-luxurious surroundings of a YMCA hostel in Wimbledon (hardly rock'n'roll, but you've got to start somewhere!). They were signed to the small Setanta label initially, before Go! Discs cottoned on to them. 'We owe everything to Setanta', says Paul, 'in fact we had sent Go! Discs a demo tape but they didn't want to know about us before Setanta came along.'

'It's like putting on a uniform for a job', Paul says about the band's outrageously eye-catching stage gear, which consists of garish purple flares, orange acrylic jumpers and decidedly naff shoes. 'We also don't have a problem worrying about stage wear', he states, 'and the clothes get us into the mood for performing.' Their song 'Fashion Crisis Hits New York' was in fact an ode to their unusual dress style. Their crazy clobber is selected for them by one of their friends back in Cork, who they describe as something of a 'lunatic'.

The band admit that they do long for their family and friends back in Cork while they are going about the business of seeking fame and fortune in foreign parts, but feel that they'd be 'nowhere' if they had remained at home where they were forced to play cover versions. 'We couldn't really get gigs there. Venues wouldn't give us gigs because they didn't know us. It was a real Catch 22 situation.'

RIGHT: *The stage name of Brian is employed by Ken Sweeney for his one-man band par excellence.*

BELOW: *The Frank and Walters, in their transfer from Cork to London, haven't lost their sense of surreal and absurd humour.*

In March 1992, they released their third EP – *Happy Busman* – through Setanta/Go! Discs. It promptly received the highly coveted accolade of Record Of The Week in the influential British pop weekly *Melody Maker*. The Frank And Walters can only continue to go from strength to strength.

Setanta is a pioneering London-based independent Irish record label established in 1989 by Irishman Keith Cullen. He felt that there were a lot of good 'left-of-centre' Irish bands who were in serious danger of compromising their style because of the Irish media's attitude towards them. The first act he signed up was Into Paradise, who later inked with Ensign, were dropped, and promptly returned to Setanta.

Other bands who were on Cullen's books included the enigmatic Dublin pop singer Brian, The Divine Comedy, The Frank And Walters and A House. He feels that up until Setanta came along, the only Irish bands who had capitalised on the quite considerable British 'indie clique' were the now sadly defunct Microdisney and The Stars Of Heaven.

Credibility is an important factor in the indie set-up, as frequent Record Of The Week accolades in the fickle British pop press save on steep advertising costs. 'We haven't made any money', maintains Keith, who runs the operation from his small South London council flat with the assistance of fellow musically devoted Irishmen Colm O'Callaghan and Fergal Hickey. 'I owe a lot, although the debts are starting to get smaller now', he says.

He feels that it is important for bands to look outside of Ireland, and derides the 'big fish in a small pond' mentality, which has beleaguered the Dublin rock scene for decades. 'If they're good, then there's no reason that they can't sell a load of records here, or in Germany or France. That's really what appeals to me. An Irish band being big in Ireland doesn't appeal to me at all. If they are then fine, if they're big everywhere else. But I don't think that only being big in Ireland is any claim to fame.'

Looking after the kids

The essence of Setanta's success, apart from the inherent quality and highly-polished individuality of the acts, is their unique communication with the young record-buying fans of Ireland, who regularly receive newsletters and free flexi discs from the company. 'Personally I get a far greater buzz from some kid writing in saying "we think you're great", instead of some journalist saying "this is wonderful" or whatever', says Keith. 'Because that journalist will crucify you or your band in two years time, whereas the people who are writing in are fans for life.'

Even if they are never to release another record (admittedly a highly unlikely scenario), U2 are assured of a prominent place in the rock history books. *Achtung Baby*, their opening salvo of the 1990s, was their finest work since 1987's *The Joshua Tree*, the album on which the 'four (Irish) boys who changed the world' finally mastered the fine art of songwriting.

No imitators

A new direction by U2 usually results in a similar activity from a myriad of younger, less-inspired bands, who unfortunately (for them) do not have limitless access to expensive recording studios or talented producers such as Daniel Lanois and Brian Eno. Interestingly enough, as with the predicted so-called 'soul explosion', attempts at imitating the *Achtung* style simply failed to materialise, and this may indicate that Irish bands are finally getting to grips with the thorny subject of originality. Or maybe *Achtung Baby* was just too darn complex and difficult to copy.

U2's next musical move will also be watched with extreme interest, but for now they are once again back on top of the pile. They may be derided by many for everything from being rich, powerful and successful, to being nothing more than musical magpies. However, through a calculated re-invention of their creative process they have proved themselves to be as adaptable and as resourceful as any long-term internationally successful rock band.

It looks as if Irish rock music in the 1990s is shooting off on a number of diverse and unrelated tangents. The jokers (Sultans Of Ping FC, Joshua Trio, Frank And Walters) and the independent bands (Into Paradise, The Stunning, The Saw Doctors, The Divine Comedy) are set for varying, degrees of success, while the superstars (U2, Enya, Sinead O'Connor) are now institutions in their own right. This is no excuse for capitalising on an established formula and not taking chances, and U2 ought to be admired for refusing to rest on their not inconsiderable laurels.

BELOW: *Why are The Pale laughing? Because they are now on the verge of international success, that's why.*

The Pale are like nothing that has ever come out of Ireland before, while the much-touted Kilkenny band My Little Funhouse belong to the rock'n'roll outlaw tradition that has rocketed controversial American band Guns'n'Roses to the top of the tree.

Others to watch include The Stunning, whose somewhat soul-based, chunky pop could win them international acclaim, if they get a decent push outside Ireland. Sweet popsters The Forget Me Nots may also be contenders, although their. tendency towards tweeness should be kept in check.

Virtual disappearing acts have done little to help the careers of either Newry's The 4 Of Us or Limerick's The Cranberries, and a higher profile will be necessary if both of these bands are to live up to great expectations. Both have coveted record deals, with Sony and Island respectively, but tours and buckets of hard work must now be on the agenda if they are to survive and prosper, although recent album releases have redressed the balance.

Something Happens have also been guilty of a long absence from the public eye, but their third album *Bedlam A Go Go* (1992) will be make or break time internationally for the Dublin four-piece who specialise in exciting, powerful pop.

Solo artists Mary Coughlan, Gavin Friday, Luka Bloom and Andy White are also front runners, but while all four can draw large crowds at home and have successfully toured both in Britain and on the continent, their continued success will rely on bigger record sales abroad. Meanwhile, established superstars Chris de Burgh and Christy Moore can only build further on their reputations and sales.

Thankfully, there is no distinctive 'Irish sound', and the sheer scope and breadth of the acts certainly makes for more exciting times. Yet the individuality of many Irish bands has occasionally been undermined by the British record companies. According to Robbie Wootton, who manages both The Hothouse Flowers and The Blue Angels (and previously looked after the affairs of hairy raggle taggle rockers The Black Velvet Band), it is not a conscious act on their part. 'They try to Anglicize all the Irish bands. The battles I've had...', he trails off.

He feels that a long-term approach is necessary for sustained success. 'The old school is gone, but there should be new goals set. With The Hothouse Flowers it was a matter of taking the next step. You'd go away and come back on a different level.'

While Wootton does believe that on a music scene which is the size of Dublin's, everybody knows what everybody else in the business is doing, he observes an acute expansion and a sharp increase in the number of bands. 'Nowadays there are just so many levels...with little bands that the UK record companies get to hear about before we do. We don't pay any attention because it's on our own doorstep.'

While the Irish music business may not be totally aware of all that is happening on its own doorstep, the British and American talent scouts are certainly well tuned in.

Maybe the main reason that the international record companies are constantly looking to Ireland for guidance is the country's refusal to blindly and unquestioningly

> *'I never thought I'd get to see America. I can't wait to go into the supermarkets and see all the stuff'*
>
> MICHELLE BURROWES
> *of The Forget Me Nots.*

ABOVE: *From a whisper to a scream. The Stunning have travelled from Galway to international regions without a great deal of hype or hysteria.*

RIGHT: *Barry Moore is Christy Moore's brother. Now known as Luka Bloom, he is fast approaching the success of his older sibling.*

follow musical trends. The 'rave' scene never really caught on to any great extent, while rap music (basically a soundtrack for black, inner city American youth) has also experienced a similar lack of mainstream interest. In 1991, Ireland's only female rap artist, MC Tyson, created an initial flutter of record company interest, but subsequently disappeared from view. There's a strong following for ethnic forms of music, with traditional, country, blues and ballads all attracting consistently good crowds in the pubs and clubs.

It is a curious fact that Ireland has yet to produce a successful hard rock band to follow in the footsteps of 1970s supremos Thin Lizzy. This is indeed baffling considering the number of fans of the genre in the country. Concerts by hard rock/heavy metal/trash rockers can now sell out by word of mouth alone through a semi-underground network.

It has been left to Belfast-born guitarist Gary Moore (ironically enough, himself more than once a member of Thin Lizzy) to fly the flag. After more than a decade of deafening decibels as a solo artist, Moore has recently rediscovered his love of the blues, and, surprisingly enough, now sells more records than he ever did before. His album **Still Got The Blues** (1990) has shifted over three million copies worldwide, while **After Hours** (1992) looks set to emulate its

success. It features the once band-hopping Moore, – a quiet unassuming person offstage – but a man who becomes possessed once he's behind his Les Paul guitar, duetting with legendary bluesmen B.B. King and Albert Collins.

'This is the kind of music I want to play all the time now', comments Moore, 'I certainly wouldn't want to go back to playing heavy metal. Previously, I'd begun to lose interest in the material I was having to record, in trying to maintain a heavy rock image and all that. But suddenly I found that by going back to the drawing board and starting from scratch I was rekindling my enthusiasm for playing.'

While Gary Moore sells records with the minimum of fuss, other acts huff and puff about how they 'deserve' a hit record because they have worked hard. But if the talent is not there then no amount of hard graft will bring chart and sales success, as many of the new wave of Irish bands have sadly discovered to their detriment.

The future is what you make it, and as invention and originality declines, the emphasis will be more than ever on shrewd marketing and image. For such a tiny country, Ireland already has its fair share of world-beaters. Measuring up to the high quality standards of U2, Van Morrison et al is not going to be easy.

> **'Jaysus, I've met them all. I even kissed Peter O'Toole'**
>
> *MARY COUGHLAN.*

ABOVE: Previously known as Blue In Heaven, The Blue Angels write occasionally divine pop music.

RIGHT: Ireland's most successful guitarist, Gary Moore, has had a pivotal role in the internationalising of Irish rock music.

A–Z OF IRISH ROCK

Biographical notes on the individuals and bands who make up the cast list of Irish rock, both past and present, together with a detailed guide to their most interesting recordings.

A HOUSE

Quirky Dublin four-piece signed by Blanco Y Negro, who released their debut album **On Our Big Fat Merry Go Round**. After the perversely non-commercial sounds of their second offering, **I Want Too Much**, the band were dropped by the label. However, they gathered their forces in 1991 to record the critically acclaimed **I Am The Greatest** album for the Irish, London-based, indie label Setanta. Fronted by singer Dave Couse, their uncompromising, thought-provoking and sometimes discordant style will always ensure them a cult following.

Recommended Listening:
I Am The Greatest (LP)
(Setanta, 1991)

AN EMOTIONAL FISH

The turbo-charged Dublin band raised many a critic's hackles when they burst on the scene in 1989 with a barrage of advance publicity. Finally managing to shake off the allegations of hype, they settled down to becoming an exciting straight-ahead noisy rock band, fronted by singer Ger Whelan, a man who gives 110 per cent on stage. Their eponymous debut album received mixed reviews, but they subsequently

ABOVE: An Emotional Fish's first album failed to live up to its pre-release hype.

exhibited potential by teaming up with Clannad's Maire Brennan for a reading of their own highly melodic 'Blue', for the *Bringing It All Back Home* TV series. With a good deal more attention to songwriting, An Emotional Fish may yet make it to deeper waters.

Recommended Listening:
Grey Matter (Single) (Mother, 1989)
Celebrate (Single) (Mother, 1990)

ASHANTI

Belfast-based three-piece band, who in 1988 were described by *Melody Maker* as 'Ireland's best kept secret'. Named after a Ghanaian tribe, they have played all over Ireland since the early 1980s. Lead guitarist Steven Boyd is the only remaining original member, with the current line-up completed by Gary Murdoch (drums) and Glenn Kingsmore (bass/vocals).

ASLAN

Signed by EMI London, Dublin band Aslan were the great white hope of the mid-1980s. With their black leather jackets, laddish humour, and hummable songs, the Finglas five-piece should have gone further than they did. Fronted by singer Christy Dignam, they eventually disintegrated, with Christy's departure highlighted in a dramatic fashion by a tabloid newspaper. The rest of the band kept the name going for some time with new singer Eamonn Doyle, but eventually called it a day. Four of the original members are now part of a band called The Precious Stones, while Christy is pursuing a career as one half of a duo with guitarist Conor Goff.

Recommended Listening:
Feel No Shame (LP) (EMI, 1987)

ATRIX, THE

As the name implied, The Atrix combined a stong theatrical element to

their quirky but memorable tunes, the most striking examples being the singles 'The Moon Is Puce' and 'Treasure On The Wasteland'. Fronted by singer John Borrowman, the four-piece were the darlings of the trendy Dublin set during the early 1980s.

Recommended Listening:
Possession (LP) (Scoff, 1981)

AUTO DA FE

Another theatrically-inclined new wave band, formed in 1980 by the charismatic Gay Woods and keyboard player Trevor Knight. Gay had been a member of both Steeleye Span and The Woods Band with her then husband Terry (later to join The Pogues), and Auto Da Fe was a radical new electronic departure for her. With Phil Lynott in the production chair and Woods' colourful live performances, the band soon built up a strong following. In 1986, after many line-up changes, Woods and Knight briefly adopted the name Operacket. While they were to occasionally reform Auto Da Fe over the next few years, the best was long behind them.

Recommended Listening:
Bad Experience (Single) (ADF, 1982)
Man Of Mine (Single) (Rewind, 1983)

AZURE DAYS

Fronted by the enigmatic Gala, the Carlow band won the Carling/*Hot Press* Band of the Year Award in 1988. They then moved to London in the hope of furthering their career, but returned to Ireland in 1991.

Recommended Listening:
Anything For You (Single)
(Grape, 1991)

BAGATELLE

In 1980, Bagatelle experienced phenomenal success with 'Summer In

Dublin', a song written by singer/piano player Liam Reilly that was seldom off the air waves. For several years, the band were huge crowd-pullers around the country, and they carried on for some time after Reilly departed the ranks for a solo career.

BAGGOT INN

Celebrated venue on Dublin's Baggot Street. In its time, it has played host to everybody from U2 and The Boomtown Rats to Phil Lynott and, during their 1991 tour, David Bowie's band Tin Machine.

BAKER, DON

Ireland's most noted exponent of the blues harmonica, Baker has, following a painful personal life, managed to combine a gutsy instrumental style with a no-nonsense, pubhouse attitude. Although he hasn't received the commercial recognition he justly deserves, Baker retains popular appeal wherever he plays in Ireland.

BIG SELF

Belfast punk/reggae band from the early 1980s. The single 'Don't Turn Around' was perhaps their finest hour, although they went on to release an album entitled *Stateless* in 1984 on the Reekus label.

BIG GERANIUMS, THE

A raggle-taggle good-time band in the old hippie tradition, with plenty of bare feet, children, dogs and fiddles in evidence. After busking in London's Covent Garden, they moved to Ireland where they were signed by Polygram Records in 1991, releasing their debut single 'Home Again' in November of that year. With members from Ireland, England and America, The Big Geraniums can truly claim an international line-up. However, with Waterboy Mike Scott no longer smelling turf in Connemara the bottom is beginning to fall out of the raggle-taggle/country scene.

BINTTII

Former Virgin Prune Binttii (known to his parents as Danny Figgis), won as much reaction for his androgynous appearance as he did from the thrash/electronic sounds he produced with his group Princess Tinymeat. The

band's first single, 'Sloblands', sharply divided opinion on his talent, while a nude Binttii on the sleeve only further fuelled the controversy. He later ventured into production, working with Dublin thrash rockers The Gorehounds. When last heard of, he was planning a new solo album.

BLACK, MARY

A member of the Black family, Mary released her eponymous debut solo album in 1983. The folk singer's distinctive voice, and soft, easy on the ear material, rapidly made her a household name. Although derided by some as a bland purveyor of housewives' choice music, there's no denying her immense popularity, which sees her selling out venues for nights on end. In 1985/6 she toured and recorded with De Dannan, before returning to her solo career. She still occasionally teams up with her family to record and perform.

Recommended Listening:
Without The Fanfare (LP)
(Dara, 1985)
No Frontiers (LP) (Dara, 1989)
Babes In The Wood (LP)
(Dara, 1991)

BLACK VELVET BAND, THE

Formed by singer/songwriter Kieran Kennedy, the band signed to Elektra, who released their debut album in 1989. Essentially comprised of Kieran, wife Maria Doyle-Kennedy and bassist Shay Fitzgerald, in late 1991 the Black Velvet Band adopted a more electric, punchier sound, leaving the acoustic raggle-taggle Bob Dylan influence behind. Maria, who is both a former member of Hothouse Flowers and a star of *The Commitments* movie, also ventured forth to sing lead vocals on several songs, having previously confined her talents to backing vocals with the band.

Recommended Listening:
When Justice Came (LP)
(Elektra, 1989)
King Of Myself (LP) (Elektra, 1992)

BLADES, THE

One of the most successful and highly-acclaimed bands of the late 1970s and early 1980s, The Blades' original line-up featured brothers Paul and Lar

Cleary on bass and guitar respectively, along with drummer Pat Larkin. Hailing from the working class South Dublin suburb of Ringsend, the trio's power-chord pop, all written by Paul Cleary, won them a huge and loyal following. Their second single – 'Ghost Of A Chance', from the album *Raytown Revisited* – is still regarded by many as possibly the greatest Irish single of all time. Line-up changes, an Ireland-only record deal, and a mod following who soon grew out of their parkas, dissipated the band's power. However, their latter stage highly-charged soul sound predated *The Commitments* movie by the best part of a decade. When last heard of, Paul Cleary was busy leading an eight-piece pub rock fun band called The Cajun Kings.

Recommended Listening:
The Last Man In Europe (LP)
(Reekus, 1985)
Raytown Revisited (LP)
(Reekus, 1986)

BLOOM, LUKA

Real name Barry Moore, the younger brother of the celebrated Christy. With a new identity, a new attitude and a new bunch of songs, Luka moved to the USA in the mid-1980s, where his impassioned acoustic performances secured him new acclaim. After winning over audiences while supporting the likes of The Pogues and The Hothouse Flowers, Bloom was soon signed to a long-term deal by Warner Brothers. He released his first album for the label in 1990. Brother Christy turned up to bang the bodhran on a couple of tracks on his 1992 album, *The Acoustic Motorbike*.

Recommended Listening:
Riverside (LP) (Reprise, 1990)
The Acoustic Motorbike (LP)
(Reprise, 1992)

BLUE ANGELS, THE

After spending much of the 1980s as the heavily-peroxided Blue In Heaven, the four members altered their name, washed out their hair, ditched their set and acquired an additional guitarist in the form of the enigmatic Quentin, a one-time fan of BIH. In August 1991, the band had the distinction of having a little-known band called Tin Machine support them in the Baggot Inn. With an impassioned leader in Shane O'Neill and subtle but powerful tunes, this band is one to watch in the 1990s.

Recommended Listening:
Candy (Single) (Solid, 1991)
Get It Back (Single) (Solid, 1991)

BLUESHOUSE

Seminal Dublin blues band from the 1960s, whose line-up featured Ed Dean (guitar), Eamon Murray (harmonica) and Dermot Stokes (piano).

BOGEY BOYS, THE

A power trio led by premier plectrum packer extraordinaire Jimmy Smith. Their single 'Friday Night' (1979) namechecked Dublin haunts like the Bailey public house. After two albums they disbanded, with Smith moving to

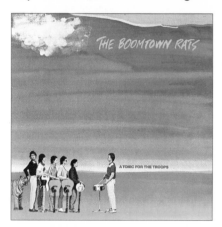

*ABOVE: **A Tonic For The Troops** gave the Boomtown Rats three hit singles.*

America where he joined up with singer Toni Childs.

Recommended Listening:
Friday Night (LP) (Chrysalis, 1979)

BOOMTOWN RATS, THE

In 1976, the outspoken Bob Geldof informed Dublin at large that his New Wave/R'n'B band The Boomtown Rats (named after a gang in Woody Guthrie's autobiography *Bound For Glory*) would sign a massive deal with a major British label. Those used to Geldof shooting his mouth off smiled benignly, but the smile soon shifted when it was announced that The Rats had signed to Phonogram for £740,000, a phenomenally high fee. Managed by former Dublin music jour-

nalist Fachtna O'Kelly, they soon stormed the British charts. From 1977 onwards, they released a series of Top 20 singles, including two Number Ones in 'Rat Trap' (1978) and 'I Don't Like Mondays' (1979). When the hits no longer kept on coming, Geldof subsequently became a household name for totally different reasons. His Band Aid/Live Aid projects helped to alleviate famine in Africa, put him on first name terms with world leaders and earned him the nickname of Saint Bob. Undeterred, he went back to The Rats, but by then the writing was on the wall, as their energy and excitement was on the wane. However, they pulled themselves together one last time for a fitting final performance at Dublin's Self Aid concert at the Royal Dublin Showground in May 1986.

Recommended Listening:
The Boomtown Rats (LP) (Ensign, 1977)
A Tonic For The Troops (LP) (Ensign, 1978)

BRADY, PAUL

Although he began his musical career in 1960s beat groups, it was as a folk/traditional performer that Strabane-born Brady first made his name. As a

*ABOVE: **Hard Station** saw Paul Brady move away from folk towards rock.*

member of The Johnstons, Planxty and one half of a duo with Andy Irvine, his powerful vocals and distinctive style helped bring Irish folk music to a wider audience. It was therefore quite a shock for some when Brady abandoned it all in 1981 and released **Hard Station**, a fully-fledged rock album that remains his finest hour. Since then

he has released several more solo soft-rock albums, suffering frequently from over-production, intensity, and, sometimes, blandness. However his success as a songwriter has been quite staggering, and Brady's tunes have been covered by a wide range of artists , including Tina Turner, Bonnie Raitt, Dave Edmunds and Santana.

Recommended Listening:
Welcome Here Kind Stranger (LP) (Mulligan, 1978)
Hard Station (LP) (WEA, 1981)
Trick Or Treat (LP) (Fontana, 1991)

BRIAN

After two highly-acclaimed singles – 'A Million Miles' and 'You Don't Want A Boyfriend' – London-based Dubliner Brian (real name Ken Sweeney) released **Understand,** his debut mini-album, on the Setanta label in 1992.

BROTHERS, THE

Fronted by Dermot and Niall Stokes, (the latter is editor of Ireland's music/current affairs magazine, *Hot Press),* The Brothers are an occasional, as yet non-gigging band who released their debut album, **Torch**, to generally positive reaction. Their sound is reminiscent of seminal American outfit, The Band, a reflection of the band's professional musicianship.

CACTUS WORLD NEWS

Formed in 1984 by Frank Kearns (guitar) and Eoin McEvoy (vocals/acoustic guitar), Cactus World News worked from the blueprint of a 'Big' sound. With Wayne Sheehy on drums and Feargal MacAindris (son of the late Eamonn Andrews) on bass they created a formidable *mélange*, that many critics unfortunately considered so much hot air. Their debut single 'The Bridge' was produced by U2's Bono for his Mother label, and following visitations from hordes of English A&R men, the band signed to MCA Records. Their 'Big' sound, the U2 connection, and uncommercial viewpoint saw the band undergo several personnel changes before they split up. In 1991, Kearns and McEvoy were again leading a band called Cactus World News, but by then it was something of a thankless task. This version also split up.

Recommended Listening:
The Bridge (Single) (Mother, 1985)

CHIEFTAINS, THE

Ireland's musical ambassadors have been on the go since the 1960s, and leader Paddy Moloney can lay claim to having played with many of the greats, including Mick Jagger, Marianne Faithful, Elvis Costello, Gary Moore and Nanci Griffith. The Chieftains'

*ABOVE: **A Chieftains Celebration**, the 1989 release from the instrumental band.*

music is the traditional sound of Ireland, with uillean pipes, whistle, fiddle and harp combining to create a backdrop which is, at times, mesmerising. Film makers have not been slow to utilise the group's talents, and they have featured on soundtracks from *Barry Lyndon* to *Treasure Island*. The band celebrated 25 years in the business in 1992. The current line-up features leader Paddy Moloney (uilleann pipes, tin whistle), Derek Bell (harp, harpsichord), Martin Fay (fiddle, bones), Sean Keane (fiddle), Matt Molloy (flute, tin whistle) and Kevin Conneff (bodhran).

Recommended Listening:
A Chieftains Celebration (LP) (RCA, 1989)
Irish Heartbeat (with Van Morrison) (LP) (RCA, 1989)
Reel Music (LP) (RCA, 1991)

CLANNAD

Now a veritable institution, Clannad (Gaelic for family) were formed in Gweedore, Donegal, in 1970. Featuring singer Maire Brennan with her brothers Paul and Ciaran, the line-up was completed by uncles Noel and

Padraig Duggan. For most of the 1970s, the band were extremely popular in Europe, while their Irish language-based sounds always ensured them a loyal following at home. In 1982, the band hit the big time when they recorded *Theme From Harry's Game* for a British TV series about an undercover agent in Northern Ireland, giving them a Top 5 British chart entry. Composed of a subtle electronic backing, along with a formidable wall of harmonies, the new Clannad sound was promptly snapped up for a major TV series on the story of Robin Hood. On their 1985 album **Macalla**, the group teamed up with U2's Bono to record 'In A Lifetime', which gave them another hit single. The group were subsequently derided for adopting West Coast soft rock influences on 1987's poorly received **Sirius**, an album which featured musicians like Russ Kunkel

*ABOVE: **Pastpresent** was a showcase for Clannad's most popular work.*

and Philip Donnelly. It was to be a short-lived experiment, and they soon reverted to the readily identifiable Clannad style.

Recommended Listening:
Fuaim (LP) (Tara, 1982)
Legend (LP) (Tara, 1984)
Pastpresent (LP) (Tara, 1989)

COMMITMENTS, THE

The fictional North Dublin band from Roddy Doyle's novel became a reality in 1990 when director Alan Parker came to the city to capture it all on celluloid. The successful 'Twelve disciples of soul' were soon catapulted to Hollywood, where lead singer Andrew Strong (Deco Cuffe in the movie) was

ABOVE: The soundtrack from the film The Commitments was hugely popular.

promptly signed by MCA Records. The then 17-year-old son of veteran Irish rocker Rob Strong set about songwriting with soul legend Lamont Dozier, in between rubbing shoulders on stage with Wilson Pickett. Also signed by MCA was Robert Arkins, who played manager Jimmy Rabbitte, and who fronts his own outfit called Housebroken. Some of the various other actors are involved with their own bands, most notably Dave Finnegan (Mickah Finnegan's Wake), Maria Doyle (The Black Velvet Band) and Glen Hansard (The Frames). Sax player Felim Gormley has toured with Andrew Strong's band, and is also featured on Rolling Stone Ron Wood's solo album. **The Commitments** soundtrack album, which featured the movie's singers, accompanied by session musicians, has sold a staggering number of copies to date. A **Commitments II** album was released in 1992.

Recommended Listening:
The Commitments (soundtrack LP) (MCA, 1991)

COUGHLAN, MARY

From Galway on the country's western seaboard, Mary Coughlan soon established herself as a flame-haired chanteuse who loved the Irish concept of having a good time called 'the craic'. Her bluesy, boozy interpretations of old classics won her acclaim at the Cork Jazz Festival in the mid-1980s. She subsequently moved to Dublin, where her outspoken views on divorce, abortion and drugs briefly threatened to eclipse the quality of her music. Her performances both at home and in Britain attracted critical acclaim. However, despite the assistance of people like Fairground Attraction's Mark E. Nevin and producer Pete Glenister on 1990's *Uncertain Pleasures*, arguably her finest album to date, she has yet to win international acclaim. After switching management in 1991, Mary took some time off to give birth in November to a baby girl. A new album with original producer Erik Visser was released in mid-1992.

*ABOVE: Mary Coughlan, with drinks, on the cover of **Under The Influence**.*

Recommended Listening:
Under The Influence (LP)
(WEA, 1987)
Uncertain Pleasures (LP)
(EastWest, 1990)
Sentimental Killer (LP)
(EastWest, 1992)

CRANBERRIES, THE

The Limerick band caused something of a stir in 1991 with the London A&R fraternity, opting in the end for Island records. Fronted by singer Dolores O'Riordan, the band still owe a heavy debt to acts like The Sundays, but their own identity may yet emerge.

DANCELINE

Pioneering Dublin-based independent label run by Pete The Roz and Eddie Joyce. With profit not the bottom line, the dynamic duo have done sterling work fostering local Irish talent. Gems among their 20-plus single releases to date include The Would Be's' 'I'm Hardly Ever Wrong', The D11 Runners' 'Yeah, Yeah!' and 'Sudden Shame' by The Way It Is.

DC NIEN

Later to become Tokyo Olympics, DC Nien combined a truly awesome live sound with a tough skinhead image. Fronted by singer Damien Gunne, the band married danceable sounds with thought-provoking lyrics, and treaded the same boards as U2 in the late 1970s and early 1980s.

DE BURGH, CHRIS

Superstar De Burgh began his career singing for his supper in Captain Americas, a hamburger restaurant on Dublin's trendy Grafton Street. Born Christopher John Davison in Buenos Aires, Argentina, in 1947, De Burgh (his mother's name) was educated in Ireland, and attended Dublin's Trinity College. Upon graduation, he went to England to embark on a musical career. He was signed by A&M, the first record company he approached in England, who released his debut album *Far Beyond These Castle Walls* in 1974. Since then the South Dublin-based De Burgh has enjoyed phenomenal worldwide success. His romantic ballads and apparently easygoing persona have won him the admiration of none other than Princess Diana, who has reportedly thrilled to his croon-erama smash hit 'Lady In Red'.

DE DANNAN

In its time, this famed Galway traditional band has included everybody from Maura O'Connell and Mary Black to Dolores Keane in its ranks. They briefly flirted with American-Irish emigration music on the single 'Molly', and Irish-influenced pop on their cover of The Beatles' 'Hey Jude'. Have since reverted to their original traditional sound and the nucleus of Alec Finn and Frankie Gavin have weathered all the storms and line-up changes.

Recommended Listening:
Anthem (LP) (Dara, 1985)
A Jacket Of Batteries (LP)
(Harmac, 1988)

D11 RUNNERS

Taking their name from the postal code of their North Dublin suburb, The D11 Runners could have stepped straight out of the pages of Roddy Doyle's *The Commitments* novel. In fact, guitar player Ken McCluskey

played bassist Derek Scully in the movie, and the band admit that their background is similar to that of the fictitious soul brothers. The D11's are very much a family affair. Formed by twin brothers Joe and Gerald Fitzgerald, Joe is married to bass player Jackie while Gerald is married to sax player Sandra. They have been plying their dance/soul sounds for five years, and one feels that they haven't yet reached their true potential.

DIGNAM & GOFF

After a stopgap solo single following his departure from Aslan, Christy Dignam linked up with ace guitarist and formidable rock warrior Conor Goff. Many questioned the match, as Goff's heavy, crashing guitar tones and Dignam's subtle and occasional fragile vocals seemed a peculiar combination. However, the band soon won a small, loyal local following.

DONNELLY, PHILIP

Ace guitar picker Donnelly played in countless Irish bands during the 1970s, including Elmer Fudd, Freddie White and the Gary Moore Band, as well as having a spell with the 1960s folk/pop star Donovan. He subsequently moved to Nashville, where he hooked up with the likes of The Everly Brothers and John Prine. Donnelly then moved back to Dublin in the late 1980s, where he formed his own band and worked as musical director for TV programmes such as *The Session*, which featured traditional Irish musicians together with American country pickers. Donnelly now lives in Cashel, County Tipperary.

Recommended Listening:
Town and Country (LP)
(Dublin Records, 1988)

DORIAN MOOD

Four-piece, Drogheda-based band of the mid-1980s who, through their sturdy power pop songs and invigorating, but occasionally frustrating, live performances, attracted a reasonable amount of positive press and audience reaction. Split up in the late 1980s.

Recommended Listening:
Can't Stand Still (LP)
(Big Mood Records, 1989)

DOYLE, ROGER

Serious avant-garde artist, who worked with 1970s improvisational groups like Supply, Demand And Curve and Jazz Therapy. In the early 1980s he formed Operating Theatre, a music-theatre group with actress Olwen Fouere. Utilising the Fairlight Computer Music Instrument (one of the first synthesisers), in 1986 he released an album entitled *Spring is Coming* on the Mother label.

DREADS, THE

Drogheda three-piece in the finest rock tradition of Johnny Thunders, New York Dolls and The Golden Horde. Fronted by singer/guitarist Ivor Lynch, the line-up has varied between a three and a four-piece. Their live performances are wild and exciting, but a debut recording has yet to materialise.

DR. STRANGELY STRANGE

Formed by Tim Booth, Tim Goulding and Ivan Pawle, Dr Strangely Strange made their live debut supporting The Incredible String Band in Dublin in 1968. A folk rock conglomerate in the classic hippie mould, the band later dabbled in psychedelia. Their second album, *Heavy Petting,* featured contributions from Gary Moore (guitar), the legendary Brush Shiels (bass) and folk hero Andy Irvine (mandolin). A product of their time, Dr Strangely Strange underwent severe line-up changes before calling it a day as the 1970s dawned.

Recommended Listening :
Kip Of The Serenes (LP)
(Island, 1969)
Heavy Petting (LP) (Vertigo, 1970)

DUBLINERS, THE

The doyens of Irish folk, The Dubliners are now an institution in themselves. Led by the white-bearded Ronnie Drew, for three decades they have achieved worldwide respect and acclaim. In the 1960s, they appeared on *Top Of The Pops* singing 'Seven Drunken Nights' and nearly 20 years later teamed up with The Pogues for a spirited reading of 'The Irish Rover' on the same show. Now essentially a four-piece featuring Ronnie Drew, Barney McKenna, Eamon Campbell

and John Sheehan, The Dubliners look set to last forever.

Recommended Listening:
The Dubliners Celebration (LP) (Harmac, 1987)
The Dubliners (LP) (EMI, 1990)
The Dubliners Collection (LP) (K Tel, 1991)

DUHAN, JOHNNY

A member of seminal 1960s Limerick band Granny's Intentions, Duhan released his first solo album in 1982. His songs have been covered by a variety of Irish artists, including Christy Moore. Now based in the west of Ireland, Duhan's most recent LP – *Family Album* – was a self-indulgent, inward-looking affair, that sold poorly.

ENERGY ORCHARD

Belfast band fronted by Bap Kennedy, brother of solo troubadour Brian. A curious hybrid of rock and raggle-taggle, Energy Orchard have toured successfully with Steve Earle, and their live performances show much promise.

ABOVE: Singer Bap Kennedy wrote all the songs for Energy Orchard's debut album.

Recommended Listening:
Energy Orchard (LP) (MCA, 1990)
Stop The Machine (LP) (MCA, 1992)

ENGINE ALLEY

Engine Alley combine quirky guitar with hummable tunes with the Marcel Marceau-type antics of singer Canice William. Also in the line-up are Eamonn Byrne (bass), Brian Kenealy (guitar), Kenneth Rice (violin) and Emmaline Fallon-Duffy (drums), and they are managed by former Radiators From Space guitarist Pete Holidai. The

*ABOVE: The **Flowerbox** EP highlighted supreme pop quirkiness from Engine Alley.*

Flowerbox EP, their debut recording on the Mother label, (1991), was produced by Steve Lillywhite (U2, The Rolling Stones, etc).

ENYA

The younger sister of the Clannad dynasty, to whose music the adjectives 'haunting' and 'atmospheric' are liberally applied. Indeed, Enya was briefly a member of the family band in the early 1980s (featuring on 1982's *Fuaim*), before she decided to strike out on a solo path. Enya's New Age hot tub sounds are not everyone's idea of what Irish rock should be, but there's no denying her success, which has seen the soft-spoken Donegal lass sell millions of albums around the world, and all this without playing one live date!

*ABOVE: Enya's mysticality was reflected on the cover of her **Watermark** album.*

Utilising layer upon layer of keyboards and vocals, her albums are painstakingly crafted over a couple of years in the home studio she shares with collaborators Nicky and Roma Ryan. While

Roma writes the lyrics, Nicky produces and engineers, and they both manage Enya. Her music is a work of true beauty.

Recommended Listening:
Watermark (LP) (WEA, 1988)
Shepherd Moons (LP) (WEA, 1991)

FANNING, DAVE

Ireland's top rock broadcaster began his career in pirate radio, but was headhunted by Radio 2 FM in the late 1970s. Since then, his nightly rock programme has enjoyed continued success, with Fanning's down-to-earth delivery one of the keys to its popularity. His *Rock Show* sessions have also helped out young up-and-coming bands, and virtually everybody who is or was anybody in Irish music has recorded a session or performed live on his show. Close to U2 through the years, Fanning has introduced them live onstage at major outdoor performances in Ireland. He is also the only radio broadcaster who can claim to have conducted a live nude interview (all five together in the all together) with the band!

FAT LADY SINGS, THE

Fronted by the gregarious Nick Kelly, The Fat Lady Sings were one of the last Irish bands to move to London to 'make it'. After a long, hard slog they finally hit paydirt with EastWest, and in 1991 released a formidable collection of well-crafted modern pop/rock tunes. Prior to this, the band had taken the unusual path of reactivating the Belfast label Good Vibrations to release their first single 'Fear and Favour' – as fine a slice of pop music as you'll find anywhere.

Recommended Listening:
Fear And Favour (Single) (Good Vibrations, 1986)
Twist (LP) (EastWest, 1991)

FATIMA MANSIONS, THE

Upon the demise of Microdisney, Cork man Cathal Coughlan formed The Fatima Mansions in 1989, taking the name from a well-known block of Dublin working class flats. As with everything Coughlan has done, passion, pride and pain were to the fore, along with some truly powerful music.

*ABOVE: The Fatima Mansions' 1989 debut album **Against Nature**.*

British newspaper *The Guardian* quite rightly described Coughlan as 'the most underrated lyricist in pop today'.

Recommended Listening:
Against Nature (LP) (Kitchenware, 1989)
Viva Dead Ponies (LP) (Kitchenware, 1990)
Bertie's Brochures (LP) (Radioactive, 1991)

FEILE

An annual three-day rock festival run in the small Tipperary town of Thurles, in central Ireland. It's an orgy of dance, drink and good times, but after 1991's event the future was threatened by clergy complaining about the excessive drinking of young people. However, in view of the valuable monetary shot in the arm that it gives the town, it looks like Feile will run and run. Artists who have played there include Van Morrison, Happy Mondays, Elvis Costello, The Pogues, Bryan Adams, Simply Red and That Petrol Emotion.

FIREFLYS, THE

Originally a power-pop four-piece from Cavan town, The Fireflys' live performances were sweaty celebrations of the genre. They subsequently succumbed to the dubious charms of second generation psychedelia and the tight haircuts and sharp suits were replaced by more generous locks and materials. Still, in the midst of it all, there was the odd gem like 'Passion Parade' crying out to make itself known to the world at large. Now disbanded, their finest hour was undoubtedly the two singles 'Judgement Day' and 'Sticks and Stones'.

FORGET ME NOTS, THE

Former buskers Michelle Burrowes and Eithne Flynn met up with ex-Classics guitarist Maurice McGrath in November 1989 and the Forget Me Nots were born. Signed by Sony Music International in August 1990, they began working on their debut album with producer Pete Wingfield. However they soon switched to Mitch Easter (REM, Suzanne Vega) and in late 1991 journeyed to America to complete recording with him. The Forget me Nots' sound is bright and breezy pop, with crisp harmonies, briskly strummed guitars and sharp, three minute tunes.

Recommended Listening:
2 Fay Wray (EP) (Soho Square, 1991)

FOUNTAINHEAD, THE

Consisting of Steve Belton and Pat O'Donnell, The Fountainhead promised a new electronic dance music for the mid-1980s. Signed by China Records, their debut dancefloor-oriented single 'Rhythm Method' was a promising start. However the lack of memorable songs on their two albums and increasingly restrained live performances signalled the death knell for the affable duo.

Recommended Listening:
The Burning Touch (LP) (China, 1986)

4 OF US, THE

The Newry band formed by brothers Brendan, Declan, and Paul Murphy, manage to combine teen appeal with well-written pop songs. The 4 Of Us started life as a studio outfit, making demos on a four track tape machine. Enormously popular in Ireland, where they have achieved huge hits with singles such as the nursery rhymelike 'Mary', and the funky 'Baby Jesus', they have as yet to make any real impact in either Europe or the USA. The band spent some of 1990 and a great deal of 1991 in hibernation, hard at work on their second album.

Recommended Listening:
Songs For The Tempted (LP) (CBS, 1989)

FRAMES, THE

Fronted by singer/songwriter Glen

Hansard, who played guitarist Outspan in *The Commitments* movie, The Frames are a curious fusion of raggle-taggle with a frantic wall of guitar rock, creating a sound not dissimilar to The Pixies. Signed by Island Records after legendary 1960s producer Denny Cordell heard their tape, the band's debut album was produced by Gil Norton of Pixies fame.

Recommended Listening:
The Dancer (Single) (Island, 1991)

FRANK AND WALTERS, THE

This Cork trio take their name from two local 'characters'. They moved to London in 1991, and their zany, unpredictable brand of fun, combined with the fact that they are also able to pen a decent pop tune, should help them go places fast. In 1991, they released two EPs on the Setanta label, before signing to Go Discs! in late autumn. Purveyors of snappy, Beatles-type guitar melodies.

Recommended Listening:
EP 1 (EP) (Setanta, 1991)
EP 2 (EP) (Setanta, 1991)
EP 3 (EP) (Setanta, 1992)

FRIDAY, GAVIN

A founder member of once-shocking art rockers The Virgin Prunes, in the late 1970s, Gavin Friday caused many a head to turn in amazement when he paraded the streets of Dublin kitted out in a dress. Out of the Prunes and in tandem with piano player The Man Seezer, Friday soon discovered his true niche as a gifted modern day cabaret singer/performer, and his Blue Jaysus cabaret club in Dublin's Waterfront was the hippest place in town during the late 1980s. While his music and persona will probably never make for mass consumption, Friday is a true original who remains uninfluenced by trends and fads. In December 1991 he hooked up with singer Maria McKee to appear at the AIDS benefit concert Red, Hot & Dance in Dublin's Olympia Theatre. The pair effortlessly stole the show. His current band, The Big No No, is led by the pianist Maurice Seezer, and features such luminaries as ex-Lounge Lizard Eric Sanko on bass and ex-Kid Creole guitarist Danny Blume.

Recommended Listening:
Each Man Kills The Thing He Loves (LP) (Island, 1989)
Adam'n'Eve (LP) (Island, 1992)

GALLAGHER, RORY

Veteran check-shirted Irish guitar hero, who first made waves in the late 1960s with his power/blues trio Taste. When Taste split up in 1970 he formed the Rory Gallagher Band – again a three-piece – and has since continued in that hard blues vein. He was mooted as a possible replacement for Mick Taylor in the Rolling Stones at the time of their **Black and Blue** album. Cork man Rory has since become a veritable institution, in between inspiring a small army of air guitar players. Gallagher has always worked hard, with constant touring and a prodigious recorded output for nearly three decades. Will always be fondly remembered as one of Ireland's premier guitar players.

Recommended Listening:
On The Boards (LP with Taste) (Polydor, 1970)
Against The Grain (LP) (Capo, 1975)
Calling Card (LP) (Capo, 1976)
Defender (LP) (Capo/Demon, 1987)
Fresh Evidence (LP) (Capo, 1990)

GELDOF, BOB

Born in Dublin in 1952, Geldof was educated at Dublin's Blackrock College. After travelling the world and working at everything from photography to journalism, he formed The Boomtown Rats in Dublin in 1975. While The Rats were in their ascendancy, Geldof met, and later married, Paula Yates, an outspoken writer/TV presenter/personality. After the trials and tribulations of Band Aid and Live Aid, Geldof took time off from both those activities and The Boomtown Rats in 1986 to record his debut solo album, **Deep In The Heart Of Nowhere**. It was a patchy affair, with the single 'This Is The World Calling' perhaps the most successful number. While his autobiography *Is That It?* sold well, and his public persona still attracted attention, it seemed that Geldof's career in music was well and truly over. However, in 1990 he surprised everybody with his second solo

album, *The Vegetarians Of Love*. An appealing mix of Irish, cajun and energetic pop music, it rekindled Geldof's songwriting flame, while drawing inspiration from Irish greats like Van Morrison and Phil Lynott.

Recommended Listening:
The Vegetarians Of Love (LP) (Phonogram, 1990)

GHOST OF AN AMERICAN AIRMAN

This Belfast rock band's rather idiosyncratic name caused their career to suffer an obvious setback at the time of the Gulf War in early 1991. They recorded an album for the Atlantic label that was never released, and are currently with Hollywood Records, with whom they have a worldwide record deal.

Recommended Listening:
Life Under Giants (LP) (Hollywood, 1992)

GOLDEN HORDE, THE

Fronted by the spectacular Simon Carmody, cartoon rockers The Golden Horde have been keeping Ireland safe for rock'n'roll for the best part of a decade. Their predominantly self-financed early recordings won them acclaim, but they delivered the killer punch in 1991, when they released their debut album proper for U2's Mother label. A glorious fusion of The Ramones, The Beach Boys, Phil Spector, Sweet, and everything else that's fine in pop, the band's live shows walk a thin line between sheer brilliance and unmitigated chaos.

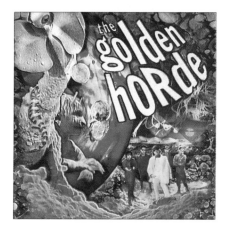

*ABOVE: A dazzling sleeve matched the music on **The Golden Horde** album.*

Recommended Listening:
The Chocolate Biscuit Conspiracy (LP) (Hotwire, 1985)
The Golden Horde (LP) (Mother, 1991)

GOREHOUNDS, THE

Dublin trash supremos from the mid-1980s. Once described as 'trash/dog rock cultists' (whatever that means!), The Gorehounds were filthy, frantic and fun. Featuring a line-up of two drummers and loud, distorted guitar, they terrorised audiences into submission with live shows that were both exciting and exhilirating.

Recommended Listening:
Semtex (LP) (Big Chief, 1989)

GRANNY'S INTENTIONS

Formed in Limerick in 1965, Granny's Intentions looked to the USA for their musical style. Influenced by everything from soul and psychedelia to The Byrds, they were signed to the Deram label in 1967 and based themselves in London. Fronted by singer Johnny Duhan, the band soon became pop stars back home in Ireland, where scenes of pandemonium ensued at their live shows. They subsequently underwent constant personnel changes, with everybody from Gary Moore to Pete Cummins (later to play with Donovan) passing through the ranks. They finally disbanded in 1971.

Recommended Listening:
Never An Everyday Thing (Single) (Deram, 1968)
Honest Injun (LP) (Deram, 1969)

HANLY, MICK

Folk/country troubadour who replaced Christy Moore in Moving Hearts. Hanly has his own soft, laid-back style, and is well capable of penning a truly original tune or two when he puts his mind to it. In the mid-1980s he fronted his own country band called Rusty Old Halo, but later returned to solo performances.

Recommended Listening:
Warts And All (LP) (Round Tower, 1991)

HARVEST MINISTERS, THE

Offbeat Dublin band, who released their debut single, 'You Do My World The World Of Good', in 1991. Their winsome melodies have attained them a cult following.

HINTERLAND

Dublin duo consisting of Gerry Leonard (guitar) and Donal Coughlan (vocals/guitar) who released their debut album, *Kissing The Roof Of Heaven*, in 1990. More at home in the studio than onstage, they have yet to make a strong impact or show their true potential.

Recommended Listening:
Kissing The Roof Of Heaven (LP) (Island, 1990)

HONEY THIEVES, THE

Formed in 1989 by guitarist Derek Turner, The Honey Thieves began their career in Dublin's famed Baggot Inn, supporting the likes of Something Happens and The Golden Horde. Their debut single 'Drive' was Single of the Fortnight in both *Hot Press* and *In Dublin* magazines, and in 1990 they won the *Hot Press* Best New Band Award. In July 1991, original lead singer Dave Lavelle departed and was replaced by Shane Walsh on vocals. Walsh made his debut a month later with the band at the Feile '91 rock festival in Thurles.

ABOVE: Several r'n'r creatures were on the cover of the Honey Thieves' 'Crawl'.

Recommended Listening:
Crawl (Single) (Liquid, 1991)

HORSLIPS

Seminal 'Celtic Rock' band from the 1970s. Horslips – Eamon Carr (drums), Johnny Fean (guitar), Barry Devlin (bass), Jim Lockhart (flute/keyboards) and Charles O'Connor (mandolin/fiddle) – recorded their debut album *Happy To Meet, Sorry To Part* in 1972, using the Rolling Stones' mobile studio. They then took on the show-bands on their own territory, and were soon packing out ballrooms around the country, an unheard of feat for a rock band. For albums like *The Tain* they dipped even further into Celtic mythology, all the time keeping up a hectic gigging schedule that took them to Europe and the USA. By the late 1970s this enormously popular and influential band had all but dropped the traditional instruments in favour of a straightforward American rock sound which, some argue, robbed them of their character and distinctiveness. In 1980, *The Belfast Gigs* album was Horslips' swan song. Carr, Fean and O'Connor joined forces briefly as The Host to record a concept album about the last witch burned in Ireland. Carr and Fean subsequently adopted less grandiose ideas and formed the Zen Alligators, a no-frills four-piece guitar band. Eamon Carr now works as a rock journalist, while Jim Lockhart produces *The Dave Fanning Show* on 2FM. Barry Devlin is involved in video/TV production while Charles O'Connor moved to London. Guitarist Johnny Fean was last heard of leading a band called The Spirit of Horslips, which reflected on the glory days of the band. Even in 1992, there are rumours of Horslips reforming for a tour. However, as far as some of the former members are concerned, such a scenario remains highly unlikely.

Recommended Listening:
Happy To Meet, Sorry To Part (LP) (Oats, 1972)
The Tain (LP) (Oats, 1973)
The Man Who Built America (LP) (Oats, 1978)

HOTHOUSE FLOWERS

In the post-U2 euphoria of the Dublin music scene many bands were labelled 'the next big thing'. Unfortunately, most were unceremoniously dumped by the British record companies that signed them. This was not the case with Hothouse Flowers. Signed by London Records, who released their debut album *People* in 1988, their 1987 single 'Don't Go' raced up the British charts, resulting in an appearance on the prestigious British chart show *Top Of The Pops*. The band had its genesis in Grafton Street in the mid-1980s when the founder members, singer Liam O'Maonlai and guitarist Fiachna O'Braonain, began to draw huge crowds while busking as The Benzini Brothers. However, they soon transferred attention to their main interest, The Hothouse Flowers, and attracted frantic A&R attention, with The Benzinis being relegated to occasional performances. With a third album now under their belts, many feel that the band's songwriter Liam O'Maonlai has yet to pen a song to equal 'Don't Go'.

Recommended Listening:
People (LP) (London, 1988)
Home (LP) (London, 1990)

HOT PRESS
Ireland's only rock magazine, which was founded by editor Niall Stokes. Celebrated its 15th anniversary in 1992. Has adopted a frequently controversial stance on Irish social issues such as divorce, religion and contraception. The publication has also championed U2 from their early days of the late 1970s, when the band was a struggling Dublin four-piece.

HOTWIRE
Independent label formed by former Horslips drummer Eamon Carr. In the mid-1980s, the roster of acts was quite impressive, with everyone from Light A Big Fire and The Golden Horde to The Stars Of Heaven and The Real Wild West releasing records. A compilation album entitled *The Weird Weird World Of Guru Weirdbrain*, which featured a collection of oddballs and fun rockers, was later released. By the late 1980s, the label was wound down as Carr concentrated on management and rock journalism.

INTO PARADISE
Formerly Backwards Into Paradise, the Dublin four-piece dropped the Backwards for a fully-fledged positive assault on the British market in the late 1980s after being signed by Ensign Records. Their 1991 album for the label was named after the band's home territory in Dublin. Dropped by Ensign in early 1992, the band are now recording for the Setanta label.

Recommended Listening:
Churchtown (LP) (Ensign, 1991)

IN TUA NUA
In Tua Nua were formed in Howth in 1982 by Ivan O'Shea and Martin Clancy. Using an unprecedented mix of traditional Irish instruments with a West Coast influence (their second single was a cover of Jefferson Airplane's 'Somebody To Love'), they soon caught the eye and the ear of U2's Bono. Their debut single, 'Coming Thru' (Adam Clayton reportedly tried to talk them out of using the American spelling!) which launched the Mother label, promised much. Its flipside, 'Take My Hand', actually had lyrics written by one Sinead O'Connor, who was briefly involved with the group before singer Leslie Dowdall joined. After a series of successful major outdoor concert performances the group were shattered when violin maestro Steve Wickham defected to The Waterboys. Pipe player Vinnie Kilduff left soon after. Undeterred, In Tua Nua recruited two new members. However, further problems struck when they were dropped by the Island record label. They pulled it out of the fire yet again by signing to Virgin, who released *Vaudeville* in 1987. The Celtic rock fusion was briefly engaging, as was lead singer Leslie Dowdall, but the lack of memorable tunes caused internal problems. Despite a moderate amount of success in Europe and the USA, the band dissolved in 1989 shortly after having completed their never-released third album.

Recommended Listening:
Coming Thru (Single) (Mother, 1984)

IRVINE, ANDY
Folk legend and former member of Planxty, who once partnered Paul Brady. Eleven years after his last solo release, Irvine returned to action with 1992's *Rude Awakening* album. As well as being a member of occasional folk 'supergroup' Patrick Street, Irvine also released a Bulgarian-sounding album called *East Wind*, which was recorded in collaboration with Irish piper Davy Spillane and various East European musicians.

Recommended Listening:
Andy Irvine/Paul Brady (LP) (Mulligan, 1976)
Rainy Sundays...Windy Dreams (LP) (Tara, 1980)
Rude Awakening (LP) (Green Linnet, 1991)

JOSHUA TRIO, THE
Popular U2 satirists, who have been known to perform like court jesters before Ireland's Fab Four themselves. Fronted by singer/guitarist and 'spiritual leader' Paul Wonderful, to 'spread the word' of Bono & Co., his antics have included arriving at the Baggot Inn dressed in flowing white robes while perched atop a donkey. In concert, the Trio ridicule everything from Bono's rap in 'Bullet The Blue Sky', to Adam's brief brush with the law, to nursery rhyme versions of other U2 songs. After some time in hibernation, The Joshua Trio re-emerged in November 1991, hot on the heels of the launch of *Achtung Baby*. They subsequently released a country and western version of 'The Fly' for the Mother label! Great in small doses.

KATMANDU
Popular Belfast band from the early 1980s, whose intriguing and entertaining rock style won them many fans in the South. Several of the highly-skilled musicians involved went on to greater things, most notably bassist Trevor Hutchinson (Waterboys) and keyboard wizard Pat Fitzpatrick, who has performed with such diverse operations as theatre orchestras and Something Happens.

KAVANA, ALIAS RON
A Cork man, who settled in London during the 1970s, and began a long-standing career on the pub rock scene. Down through the years he has toured and recorded with everybody from Elvis Costello and the Pogues to Alexis Korner and Fairport Convention's Sandy Denny. Only formed his own band as recently as 1987, and since then he has built up a loyal and dedicated following. Kavana describes his music as country and Irish. He has experimented successfully with all forms, including rap, ceilidh, country, African and blues.

Recommended Listening:
Think Like A Hero (LP)
(Chiswick, 1989)
Coming Days (LP) (Chiswick, 1991)
Home Fire (LP)
(Special Delivery, 1991)

KEANE, DOLORES

West of Ireland singer whose style switches quite effortlessly between traditional, country and soft-rock. However both Keane and her fans are probably most at home with the type of traditional Irish music on which she was reared.

Recommended Listening:
Dolores Keane and John Faulkner
(LP) (Gael Linn, 1983)
Lion In A Cage (LP)
(Round Tower, 1989)

KENNEDY, BRIAN

Honey-voiced Belfast singer, who moved to London as part of the band Energy Orchard. After releasing his own solo album, Kennedy teamed up with ex-Fairground Attraction songwriter Mark E. Nevin to form a band called Sweetmouth. This band aside, they both intend to concentrate on their respective solo careers.

Recommended Listening:
Goodbye To Songtown
(LP by Sweetmouth) (BMG, 1991)

KING, PHILIP

In 1991, King, a member of veteran folk-rock band Scullion, finally saw his ambitious *Bringing It All Back Home* project reach fruition. A TV series, with an accompanying book, it traced the journey of Irish music to the USA and back. Hence the title. Opinions were divided on some of the claims put forward, because while there was no denying some influence, the scale on which it was presented was certainly open to doubt. Artists appearing included everyone from U2 and The Hothouse Flowers to The Everly Brothers and Elvis Costello. King also co-authored 'I Am Stretched On Your Grave', which was recorded by Sinead O'Connor on her *I Do Not Want What I Haven't Got* album.

LIGHT A BIG FIRE

Signed by the English label Siren in 1986, Dublin band Light A Big Fire set about expanding their sound and in the process lost what many believe was their true charm. With extra guitar and keyboards in the line-up their new American sound moved even further away from the ragged glory of their early gigs and recordings, which centred on Tom McLaughlin's deft singing and guitarist Pete Dench's highly distinctive style. Their 1987 album *Surveillance* caused ripples instead of waves and upon completion of recording their second album (which was never released) McLaughlin promptly quit the band.

Recommended Listening:
Gunpowders (mini-LP)
(Hotwire, 1985)
Surveillance (LP) (Siren, 1987)

LIR

Reputedly a progressive rock band for the 1990s, Lir caused quite a stir when they performed at the 1991 New Music Seminar in New York but have yet to capitalise on the publicity.

LUNNY, DONAL

Well-respected musician/producer, who founded folk-rock fusionists Moving Hearts. A childhood friend of Christy Moore, the pair grew up in Newbridge, County Kildare, and both were members of the legendary Irish folk band Planxty. Lunny subsequently produced much of Moore's solo work. In December 1991, Lunny put together an all-star band to back Sinead O'Connor for a benefit concert in Dublin's National Stadium.

Recommended Listening:
Planxty (LP) (Polydor, 1972)
The Storm (LP by Moving Hearts)
(Tara, 1985)

LYNOTT, PHIL

On 4 January 1986 it all caught up on former Thin Lizzy leader Phil Lynott when he died at 34 years of age after collapsing on Christmas Day from kidney and liver failure. Ironically, at the time Lynott had been talking with Lizzy drummer Brian Downey about reforming the band. Two years previously they had disbanded, with Lynott wanting to move on to new things. This involved a brief spell fronting an outfit called Grand Slam, as well as collaborations with both Paul Hardcastle ('19') and former Lizzy axeman Gary Moore ('Out In The Fields'). While Thin Lizzy's macho strut was loud, dangerous and exciting, it frequently obscured the more melodic, mellow side of Lynott's songwriting. This is best evidenced on his two solo albums, *Solo In Soho* (1980) and *The Philip Lynott Album* (1982). A true great of Irish rock, Phil Lynott was one of the first Irish superstars who made it on his own terms. Every year, his legacy is celebrated with a special memorial concert in Dublin on the anniversary of his death.

Recommended Listening:
Solo In Soho (LP) (Vertigo, 1980)
The Philip Lynott Album (LP)
(Vertigo, 1982)

MACGOWAN, SHANE

Pogues' founder, figurehead, singer and songwriter MacGowan departed from the band in 1991 amidst much brouhaha. His place was taken by former Clash singer Joe Strummer, and MacGowan announced plans to form a new band with ex-Thin Lizzy guitarist Brian Robertson. However, nothing further was heard about this somewhat disquieting alliance, and MacGowan is reported to be working on songs for a solo album. If it materialises it promises to be captivating, as despite all the problems with the demon drink, MacGowan, who was born in London of Irish parents, has proved himself to be a songwriter *par excellence*. Even if he never manages to record another note, his superb songs like 'Fairytale Of New York' and 'Summer In Siam' will bear testimony to his greatness.

Recommended Listening:
The Best Of The Pogues (LP)
(Warners, 1991)

MALE CAUCASIANS

Northern Irish band who made a small but important impression in the early 1980s with their superficial, but attractive, brand of Television-inspired, wired-to-the-moon pop/rock. Have since disappeared without trace.

MAMA'S BOYS

Forget the soppy name – County

Fermanagh's Mama's Boys (Pat, Johnny and Tommy McManus) were one of Ireland's most traditionally rockist outfits. Despite the three brothers' traditional folk background – Pat and Johnny won the All Ireland championships for fiddle and tin whistle, respectively – the band soon settled for guitars and drums. Originally known as Pulse, the trio developed a large cult following in Belfast, their utilisation of the more melodic side of heavy metal gaining them fans among both the public and media. Throughout their career they were beset by personal problems – guitarist Pat was once kidnapped by unknown assailants on his way from a gig, and their drummer, Tommy, was forced to intermittently jettison his band role due to recurring bouts of leukaemia. Although popular both home and abroad, Mama's Boys lost out in the international market because of their identikit hard rock sound and image.

Recommended listening:
The Official Album (LP)
(Pussy,1980)
Plug It In (LP) (Pussy, 1982)
Growing Up The Hard Way (LP)
(Jive, 1987)

MERRIGAN, SARAH

1991 was the year that 18-year-old Sarah Merrigan was pushed into the limelight. Invariably hyped as the 'new' Sinead O'Connor (whatever that meant), Sarah attracted a plethora of record company interest but ended the year with nothing resolved. One suspects that her vastly eclectic range of songs didn't click with those record companies who wanted to mould her into something she clearly didn't want to be. She's precocious, intelligent and talented, and we should be hearing more from Sarah Merrigan.

MICRODISNEY

Formed in Cork in the late 1970s following the explosive inspiration of punk. Main members were Cathal Coughlan (see Fatima Mansions) and Sean O'Hagan. Other original members included Mick Lynch and Rob McKahey (see Stump). The initial sound of Microdisney was both anarchic and cathartic, with Coughlan's rantings typifying the frustration of an angst-ridden young Irishman. Come

the 1980s, their sound gained from a more melodic input and carefully subversive lyrics from O'Hagan and Coughlan respectively. Through vari-

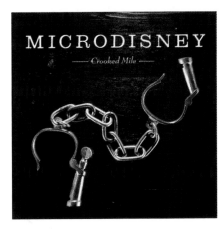

ABOVE: Microdisney's **Crooked Mile**. *Intense songs for intense listeners.*

ous classic albums for both Rough Trade and Virgin, Microdisney fashioned a marvellous form of acerbic pop music. The band split up due to lack of commercial interest and internal disputes in the late 1980s. Definitely one of Ireland's most important bands.

Recommended listening:
We Hate You South African Bastards (LP) (Rough Trade, 1984)
The Clock Comes Down The Stairs (LP) (Rough Trade, 1985)
Crooked Mile (LP) (Virgin, 1987)

MOONDOGS, THE

Belfast-based teen punk group who, along with Rudi, Protex, The Tear jerkers and The Undertones, defined the principles of Northern Irish punk rock. A band very much in the pretty boy, teen dream mould, the Moondogs none the less inspired as much as they irritated.

Recommended listening:
She's Nineteen (Single)
(Good Vibrations, 1979)

MOORE, CHRISTY

Seminal figure in Irish traditional and folk music. Born in the mid-1940s, Moore left Ireland for England in the mid-1960s following a prolonged strike at the bank where he worked. After immersing himself in the wide accessibility of the English folk circuit he returned to Ireland in 1970 with a vision of what Irish folk music could

and should be. With Donal Lunny, Andy Irvine and Liam Og O'Flynn – the core of musicians on Moore's legendary folk debut, **Prosperous**, Moore formed the groundbreaking Planxty in the early 1970s. Following almost a decade in both band and solo guises, Moore founded Moving Hearts, a justifiably acclaimed Irish group that utilised elements of traditional, jazz and rock music in its dynamic ensemble style of playing. In 1982, Moore once again decided to go solo, a career move which has sustained him admirably to date. Moore remains one of Ireland's best loved and most innovative singer/songwriters. Although firmly entrenched in the folk-singing tradition, he has shown his awareness of current trends by covering songs by seminal Dublin band, Radiators From

ABOVE: Fine 1980s and 1990s folk songs filled **The Christy Moore Collection**.

Space ('Faithful Departed') and, none too surprisingly, The Pogues ('A Pair Of Brown Eyes'). A heart attack in the late 1980s proved to be a minor setback. Moore looks set to spearhead the folk movement in the 1990s much as he did in the 1970s.

Recommended listening:
Prosperous (LP) (Tara, 1972)
Planxty (LP) (Polydor, 1973)
Rainy Sundays... Windy Dreams (LP) (Tara, 1980)
Moving Hearts (LP) (WEA, 1981)
Ordinary Man (LP) (Demon, 1985)
Unfinished Revolution (LP) (WEA, 1987)
Smoke And Strong Whiskey (LP) (Newberry, 1991)
The Christy Moore Collection (LP) (WEA, 1991)

MOORE, GARY

Belfast-born Gary Moore picked up an electric guitar at 11 years of age, heard Jeff Beck in the early 1960s, and hasn't looked back since. He joined legendary Irish rock band Skid Row in the late 1960s, already an inspired guitar veteran at 16. Played with other seminal Irish bands (Granny's Intentions, Dr Strangely Strange); formed the transitory Gary Moore Band, then joined Thin Lizzy. Left soon after to join well respected British jazz/rock fusion group, Colosseum, for over three years (for Moore a very long time in one band!) Subsequently rejoined Thin Lizzy for live shows and their traditionally-influenced *Black Rose* album. Then travelled to Los Angeles to form well-liked hard rock band, G-Force. Further associations with both Thin Lizzy (Moore appeared on their 1983 farewell tour) and Phil Lynott (a duet on the hit single, 'Out In The Fields', in 1985) ensued amidst various solo projects. A likeable and steady-as-granite figure in Irish rock music, Moore appears to have gained more respect outside Ireland than he has at home. A rock maverick, Moore has a strong Celtic spirit shining through his diamond-hard guitar playing.

Recommended listening:
Back On The Streets (LP) (MCA, 1978)
Victims Of The Future (LP) (10/Virgin, 1983)
Run For Cover (LP) (10, 1985)
Wild Frontier (LP) (10, 1987)
After The War (LP) (Virgin, 1989)
After Hours (LP) (Virgin, 1992)

MORRISON, VAN

Just about the most unlikely looking pop/rock icon there is, Van Morrison is justifiably Ireland's greatest living legend. Born in Belfast on 31 August, 1945, Morrison's family background was steeped in jazz, blues and country. He left school in the late 1950s to join local showband, the Monarchs, but became tired both of their work schedule and of continually playing cover versions. Travelled to London in 1963 but returned home weeks later. The winter of that year Morrison met guitarist Bill Harrison and together they formed Them. In 1964, Them went to London on recording contract deal from Decca. Following respectable commercial success, Them split up in 1966 due to internal and financial problems. From Morrison's debut solo album, *Blowin' Your Mind* in 1967 to his 1991 double album, *Hymns To The Silence*, he has consistently and stubbornly refused to kowtow to anything except his own iron will. His albums have been both praised to the heights *(Astral Weeks)* and critically

*ABOVE: One of the best rock albums ever: Van Morrison's **Astral Weeks**.*

disposed of *(A Period Of Transition)*, but his standing as one of rock music's great figures remains undisputed. Morrison is also the only Irish rock musician who continually invests his music with a sense of place and Celtic mysticism that remains true to his unique vision. Some of his material suffers from quasi-religious pretension and can be both infuriating and shallow, but, like all truly important artists, his classic works overshadow any negative critical prejudice.

Recommended listening:
Astral Weeks (LP) (Warners, 1968)
Moondance (LP) (Warners, 1969)
St Dominic's Preview (LP) (Warners, 1972)
It's Too Late To Stop Now (LP) (Warners, 1974)
Veedon Fleece (LP) (Warners, 1974)
Wavelength (LP) (Warners, 1978)
Beautiful Vision (LP) (Mercury, 1982)
A Sense Of Wonder (LP) (Mercury, 1985)
No Guru, No Method, No Teacher (LP) (Mercury, 1986)
Irish Heartbeat (LP) (Mercury, 1988)
Avalon Sunset (LP) (Polydor, 1989)
Hymns To The Silence (LP) (Polydor, 1991)

MOTHER

Irish-based record label set up in the mid-1980s by U2. Initially castigated by critics as being merely a label to help their personal friends get a foothold in the international record market. Early signed bands (Cactus World News, In Tua Nua) tended to suffer from lack of individuality, but latterly several groups of both power, style and diversity (The Golden Horde, Engine Alley) have shown that Mother is finally getting its act together. In retrospect, Mother was a genuinely altruistic move on U2's part to showcase exclusively Irish bands. Scotland's The Painted Word was the label's sole non-Irish act.

MOVING HEARTS

Founded in early 1981 by Christy Moore and Donal Lunny, Moving Hearts were an innovative group that managed to successfully fuse folk and rock, and also to imbue those forms with jazz and ethnic mixes. Their debut album, *Moving Hearts*, became, on its release in 1981, the biggest selling indigenous album. Subject matter on the album was overtly political, music was expertly played and developed a new musical category within the Irish traditional framework. Group disbanded in 1984 due to financial difficulties (running the band along co-operative lines, without a manager as such, hadn't helped) and fragmented personnel involvement (Moore's place as vocalist was taken over by Mick Hanly, who in turn was replaced by Flo McSweeney). Reformed in 1985 for one instrumental album. They remain one of Ireland's top pioneering bands.

Recommended listening:
Moving Hearts (LP) (WEA, 1981)
Moving Hearts Live (LP) (WEA, 1983)
The Storm (LP) (Tara, 1985)

MY BLOODY VALENTINE

Irish/English band who experiment in controlled guitar noise and soaring melody lines, My Bloody Valentine are in the forefront of screeching, sonic guitar attack. Left Dublin for London soon after they formed, feeling the need to meet like-minded individuals and suitable non-conformists. The band are treated with scant regard by the majority of the Irish music media who seem to be suspicious of their unusual work ethic, an ethic that has since spawned a vast number of imitators. Very influential in their own barbed way.

Recommended listening:
Isn't Anything (LP) (Creation, 1988)
Loveless (LP) (Creation, 1991)

NUN ATTAX
Pranksters who paved the way for a certain style of musical lunacy peculiar, it would transpire, to bands from Cork. Fronted by the seriously madcap Finbarr Donnelly (who tragically died in a boating accident in the late 1980s), Nun Attax created a blueprint for charming awkwardness that continues to this day in bands such as The Frank And Walters (also from Cork).

O'CONNELL, MAURA
Crystal clear vocalist from Ennis, County Clare, Maura O'Connell first came to prominence with traditional group De Danann during the late 1970s and early 1980s. She left De Danann in late 1983 to follow a solo career. Her integration of traditional music and American ethnic musical styles makes for a lasting listening impression, although she suffers from continual comparison with other Irish female singers who straddle the same musical forms.

Recommended listening:
Maura O'Connell (LP) (Ogham, 1983)
A Real Life Story (LP) (Warners, 1991)

O'CONNOR, SINEAD
Precocious and very talented female singer, O'Connor has, in her short recording career, put together a body of work that older and more experienced colleagues can only envy. In the space of four years – and not including her nascent career experiments with Irish bands, In Tua Nua and Ton Ton Macoute – O'Connor has fashioned a commercially successful anti-style in both attitude and music. While her

public announcements on various topics (Ireland, abortion, religion) have both irritated and concerned her critics and fans, the music on her two acclaimed albums has been received with largely widespread fervour. An international profile was foisted upon her when the single, 'Nothing Compares 2 U', a Prince composition, took off worldwide, effectively making her a household name. Fame does not rest easily on her shoulders, however, and in the latter part of 1991 O'Connor professed a growing disillusionment with the music business and her part in it. It's unlikely, though, that she will leave it for good – she's too talented and has too much to say to content herself with a film career, her purported other career preference.

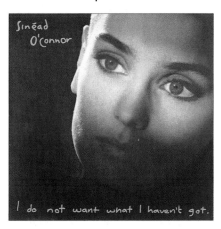

ABOVE: International Number 1 album: I Do Not Want What I Haven't Got.

Recommended listening:
The Lion And The Cobra (LP) (Ensign, 1987)
I Do Not Want What I Haven't Got (LP) (Ensign, 1990)

OUTCASTS, THE
A much underrated Northern Irish punk rock band. The group's aggressive image of hedonistic and deranged skinheads was matched by their uncompromising music, which was a lethal combination of pop tunes and scratchy fast punk. Their live act usually teetered on the brink of violence, the band's natural aggression spilling over into the music. The Outcasts released several singles and an album on the Belfast-based Good Vibrations label, but despite solid critical approval, disappeared from view as the mid-1980s approached.

Recommended listening:
Self Conscious Over You (LP) (Good Vibrations, 1979)

PALE, THE
One of Ireland's curiosities, The Pale don't fit the standard brief for Irish rock bands. Although both their image and music seem contrived (skinhead haircuts, distinct European rhythms), there's something intuitive and natural about the band. After much speculation, they signed a major record deal in late 1991 with A&M records. Managed by Columb Farrelly, an ex-member of Ton Ton Macoute. No vinyl (or CD) product as yet, although *Hot Press* magazine had a giveaway flexi-disc of a Pale song – 'Moon' – in their Christmas 1991 issue. Expect this to become a collector's item.

PARANOID VISIONS
Dublin's outsiders in the race for commercial and critical plaudits, stubborn punk rockers Paranoid Visions remain a band to be both respected (for their intransigent stance in the face of mediocrity) and abused (their *naïveté* at thinking that their punk stance could shake the musical establishment). The band's brand of no-nonsense and often turgid 1977-trapped punk rock indicates a perverse and wilful refusal to adapt. In other words, they hate U2.

PARTISANS, THE
After the Blades split up in 1986, lead singer and vocalist Paul Cleary formed the take-it or leave-it Partisans, a band that almost succeeded in emulating the winning creative formula of Cleary's former outfit. Dogged by the conflict between artistic worth and commercial insignificance, The Partisans went through various line-up changes with Cleary at the helm. Undoubtedly one of Ireland's most important songwriters, of late Cleary has undermined his own genuine creativity and profile by his absence from the Irish music scene.

Recommended listening:
Impossible (LP) (Hotwire, 1987)

PLANXTY
Formed by Christy Moore, Andy Irvine, Liam Og O'Flynn and Donal Lunny in the early 1970s, Planxty became one of Ireland's most influen-

tial traditional bands. The band explored the purity of traditional Irish music, most notably captured on their eponymous debut album. Paul Brady joined in 1974, settling in along with another new member, Johnny Moynihan, who replaced Donal Lunny. Christy Moore left in 1975 to pursue a solo career and Planxty broke up at the end of 1975. They reformed in 1979 much to the enthusiasm of traditional music fans, but split up soon after. Planxty continue to be spoken of in reverent terms by traditional music fans and historians as being one of Ireland's most significant traditional groups.

Recommended listening:
Planxty (LP) (Polydor, 1973)

POGUES, THE
Created in North London in 1983 by Tipperary-born, disaffected punk rocker Shane MacGowan, The Pogues were a much needed shot in the arm for those who were tired of a maudlin, sentimentalised version of Irish traditional music. To many, they portray a vision of an Ireland that is working-class, drunken and violent, but over the years the band have invested their songs with far more melody and maturity than their initial critics would have given them credit for. Along the way,

*ABOVE: **Rum, Sodomy And The Lash** was The Pogues' finest, most chaotic hour.*

The Pogues have enlisted the help of Terry Woods, noted Irish folk artist, and Philip Chevron, ex-lead guitarist/vocalist with Radiators From Space. Their largely shambolic live performances have always hinged on the x-factor of mercurial lead singer and

acclaimed lyricist, MacGowan, while their album releases have veered between the classic – **Rum, Sodomy And The Lash** and the mediocre – **Peace And Love**. In late 1991, MacGowan's increasing dependence on alcohol resulted in him being asked to leave the band. He was replaced by ex-Clash frontman Joe Strummer on a semi-permanent basis. The possibility of MacGowan being involved with the band again, in either performance or songwriting cannot be ruled out.

Recommended listening:
Rum, Sodomy And The Lash (LP) (Stiff, 1984)
Poguetry In Motion (EP) (Stiff, 1985/Warners, 1991)
If I Should Fall From Grace With God (LP) (Stiff, 1988)
Hell's Ditch (LP) (Warners, 1990)
The Best Of The Pogues (Compilation LP) (Warners, 1991)

POWER OF DREAMS
Powerhouse Dublin group who specialise in writing songs of great pop structure albeit with a brutal and forceful playfulness. Fronted by flame-haired Craig Walker, Power Of Dreams have – like many other native bands – the capabilities to break down the international commercial barriers that have dogged Irish acts for a number of years. The image, the songs, the attitude – they're all there. The Japanese, apparently, are ape-crazy for the band.

Recommended listening:
Immigrants, Emigrants And Me (LP) (Polydor, 1990)
To Hell With Common Sense (LP) (Polydor, 1992)

PRAYER BOAT, THE
This band from Blessington, County Wicklow occupy a similar musical terrain to that of Van Morrison: spacey, Celtic, mystical and abstract. As yet, the band have not harnessed their sound into anything remotely as cohesive as their mentor's.

Recommended listening:
Oceanic Feeling (LP) (RCA, 1991)

PRUNES, THE
A continuation of The Virgin Prunes, this band have thoroughly dispensed

with the shock-horror visuals and ambient-Gothic tones, fashioning in their place a solid but likeable mainstream rock guitar sound not unlike The Jesus And Mary Chain. The Prunes, however, are nowhere near as cataclysmic a force as they were in their Virgin days.

Recommended listening:
Blossoms And Blood (LP) (New Rose, 1991)

RADIATORS FROM SPACE
Although The Boomtown Rats were perceived to be Ireland's first punk rock band, it was really The Radiators From Space who could lay claim to that title. Formed in the flowering of punk in 1977, the band gained a reputation for crystalising a certain disaffection amongst sectors of the Irish youth. Their first album, **TV Tube Heart,** was full of guitar-driven, anthemic attacks on various subjects, notably media brainwashing. In 1979, as The Radiators, they released their second album, **Ghostown**, a classic Irish rock record that was sadly overlooked by the British press. Their erstwhile lead guitarist, Philip Chevron, is now esconced in The Pogues, while The Radiators' ex-lead singer, Steve Rapid (Steve Averill) is a design consultant with U2, amongst others, on his clientele list. Pete Holidai, ex-guitarist, now manages Mother hopefuls, Engine Alley.

Recommended listening:
TV Tube Heart (LP) (Chiswick, 1977)
Ghostown (LP) (Chiswick, 1979)

REAL WILD WEST
Short-lived Irish rock band who specialised in Beefhartian rhythms and cracked vocals, courtesy of Charlie Rafferty. An oddity at the best of times, in a live setting the band could be as sharp as glass and as fragile as a twig. File under 'misunderstood'.

RHYTHM KINGS, THE
In an earlier incarnation – and slightly different personnel – were known as Rocky De Valera And The Grave Diggers. The common bond was lead singer, Ferdia MacAnna, a tall, gangling individual with a love of rhythm'n'blues and 1950's rock'n'roll. Essentially a live

band, The Rhythm Kings won the hearts of Irish people nationwide with their professional and infectious brand of pop/rock/r'n'b. They split up in 1983, following their debut album release and, since then, no r'n'b type band has come close to matching their popularity.

Recommended listening:
Setting Fire To My Heart (LP) (Scoff, 1983)

ROCK GARDEN, THE
Not a band, but a venue, and one that has opened up an entirely new vista on Irish rock music. Situated in Dublin, in the Temple Bar area of the city, The Rock Garden – affiliated to the London venue of the same name – has been instrumental in the breakthrough of many up-and-coming Irish rock groups. It's easily the best-equipped mid-size venue in the city, thereby giving even the most rudimentary of outfits a boost heretofore missing on the Irish circuit.

RUDI
Formed in the late 1970s, Rudi were the quintessential Northern Irish punk band with a deep-rooted understanding of how to integrate that form with pop music. Released a couple of singles that have stood the test of time. Their best recording was 'Big Time', a resounding slab of all that is perfect in a powerful pop song. Split up in the early 1980s.

Recommended listening:
Big Time (Single) (Good Vibrations, 1978)
When I Was Dead (Single) (Jamming! Records, 1979)

RUEFREX
Formed in 1977, this Belfast group were much more political than contemporaries Stiff Little Fingers could ever be. The band signed to the Belfast-based Good Vibrations label in the same year as their formation, but it took them almost a decade to finally release an album (on the Stiff label). Ruefrex had its trump card in Paul Burgess, a songwriter of immeasurable power and substance, especially when it came to highlighting his country's war-torn plight. Powerful songs, alas, didn't bring the band their deserved

success and they split up shortly after the album's release.

Recommended listening:
Flowers For All Occasions (LP) (Stiff, 1985)

SACK
Previously known as Lord John White, the band changed their name to Sack due to media and public difficulty with image identification. The band's quite shocking brand of kinetic dance music, however, has mutated over the years into something both really interesting and appealing. Bigger and better things are definitely expected.

Recommended listening:
Jungleburger (As Lord John White) (EP) (Lemon, 1990)

SAW DOCTORS, THE
In 1991, undoubtedly the Irish band of the year. They came from virtually nowhere in late 1989 to national megastardom in the space of months. Their brand of rustic/traditional rock'n'pop has divided not their multitude of fans but the country's critics and social commentators. Some see The Saw

ABOVE: The Saw Doctors put their fathers on the cover of their debut album.

Doctors as the Irish band to bring back certain social values into a musical and social agenda that seems preoccupied with hedonistic rock'n'roll. Others view them as country bumpkins (their homestead is Tuam, County Galway; far removed from the Dublin power-base) who got lucky through their best-selling single of 1991, 'I Useta Love Her'. Regardless of how they're perceived by the pundits, the public

love them. The band, however, do possess an anti-star, lowest common denominator appeal that might, in the long term, be their downfall.

Recommended listening:
If This Is Rock And Roll I Want My Old Job Back (LP) (Solid, 1990)

SCOFF
Record label jointly set up by ex-Stepaside lead singer and Irish pub rock originator Deke O'Brien and publisher Johnny Lappin. Between the late 1970s and mid-1980s, Scoff did as much for the promotion and development of Irish rock as Danceline or Solid are doing now.

SCULLION
Acoustic folk/soft rock band which was formed during the late 1970s. Scullion have a special place in Irish music by virtue of their mature eclecticism and high ambitions. The nucleus of Sonny Condell and Philip King has managed to absorb various line-up changes, but the essential sound of the band rotates around Condell and King. Throughout the 1980s, the band split up and re-formed many times. Mercurial talents, Scullion's trademark of accomplished adult folk/soft rock is best exemplified by their 1986 single, 'Carol'. Still around and playing gigs in one form or another.

Recommended listening:
Balance And Control (LP) (WEA, 1981)
Spin (LP) (Dara, 1986)

SETANTA
A London-based, Irish-affiliated independent record label, Setanta has been instrumental in the careers of Irish rock bands such as Into Paradise, A House and The Frank And Walters. Founded by Keith Cullen, Setanta is an important adjunct to the 'major' music industry labels as well as being something of an inspiration to those Irish rock bands who feel alienated by record company bureaucracy.

SHAINE
Irish band with some pretensions to seriousness and social comment within their songs. Shaine have a tendency to gloss over these topics with a vaguely middle-of-the-road rock sound and,

although slightly tougher in a live context, their songs will have to undergo radical treatment if they are to make a bigger impact.

Recommended listening:
Dreamtown (Single) (Lime, 1991)

SHANNON, SHARON

Not so much rock'n'roll as Irish traditional music played with a vaguely rock'n'roll aesthetic, Sharon Shannon paved the way for a form of music which would use the approach of the two styles. Discovered by Waterboy Mike Scott, Sharon has now found her own niche in Irish music circles. Will always be afforded critical and public respect for her music in Ireland and elsewhere, although international commercial success seems unlikely.

ABOVE: **Sharon Shannon** *– more smoothly blended Irish traditional music.*

Recommended listening:
Sharon Shannon (LP) (Solid, 1991)

SHARKEY, FEARGAL

Ex-lead singer of pristine pop/punk Irish group The Undertones, Sharkey commenced a solo career in late 1983 with 'Never Never', an electro-pop single with Vince Clarke (ex-Depeche Mode). Since then, he has continued to increase his profile by releasing idiosyncratic, if mannered, slightly soul-influenced albums. Never a strong songwriter, Sharkey has had more success with cover versions of songs that suit his distinct and sophisticated style of singing. Has never achieved the same degree of critical appreciation as he did when in The Undertones. Naturally enough, this does not appear to bother him. A maverick talent.

ABOVE: **Songs From The Mardi Gras.** *Studied singing from Feargal Sharkey.*

Recommended listening:
Feargal Sharkey (LP) (Virgin, 1985)
Songs From The Mardi Gras (LP) (Virgin, 1991)

SHIELS, BRUSH

Founder member of Skid Row, one of Ireland's most innovative bands in the 1960s. Since the mid-1970s, Shiels has become, in the minds of the Irish public, more of a media personality than a rock musician. Still gigging extensively, he is a well-known sight on Irish television and stage where, with his distinctive beret atop bald head, he continues to play deranged 1960s influenced guitar. In the mid-1980s', he released 'Old Pal', a moving tribute to his long time friend, Phil Lynott, an excellent song that is in stark contrast to his other material.

Recommended listening:
Old Pal (Single) (CMR, 1986)

SKID ROW

Vastly influential Irish rock band who, along with Taste and Thin Lizzy, placed Ireland on the international music map in the late 1960s/early 1970s. Founded in 1967 by Brendan 'Brush' Shiels, Skid Row were a group unprecedented in those days by virtue of their experimentation and musical approach. Floating members of the band during those early years included Phil Lynott and Gary Moore. Achieved critical and commercial acclaim in both Europe and the USA, with the band's unusual but effective stew of progressive rock, blues and psychedelia proving a unique blend of styles. Recorded two excellent albums prior to splitting up in the early 1970s. Will be remembered as

one of the most important of seminal Irish rock bands.

Recommended listening:
Skid (LP) (CBS, 1970)
34 Hours (LP) (CBS, 1971)

SOLID

Irish record label founded in the late 1980s. Has given tremendous support to many Irish rock bands by releasing one-off singles. The label's roster reads like a shopping list of great-to-good-to-middling Irish rock groups. Profile of label boosted in 1991 by their biggest-selling act, The Saw Doctors, whose debut album, **If This Is Rock And Roll, I Want My Old Job Back**, became Ireland's best-selling album of that year. In late 1991, initiated a sister label, Liquid.

SOME KIND OF WONDERFUL

A Dublin/Dundalk outfit from the late 1970s that – contrary to the punk spirit of the times – formulated a sound that drew on funk rhythms and Eastern influences. They lived a short but exotic existence and split up in the early 1980s, having left a lasting impression on the gig-goers of Ireland.

Recommended listening:
D'You Read My Letter (Single) (Reekus, 1980)

SOMETHING HAPPENS

Formed in mid-1980s, Something Happens – from lowly beginnings as quasi-REM devotees – soon became one of Ireland's most inventive and exciting fast pop/rock bands. Initially

ABOVE: Something Happens' 1992 pure guitar pop album **Bedlam A Go Go.**

the band had a disposition towards finding (and forcing) a fun element in everything, but they soon grew tired of this and started to experiment in both song structure and attitude on their second album. A superb pop band, Something Happens have yet to break into the commercial heart of the music industry, but it certainly hasn't been for the want of talent.

Recommended listening:
Been There, Seen That, Done That (LP) (Virgin, 1988)
Stuck Together With God's Glue (LP) (Virgin, 1990)
Bedlam A Go-Go (LP) (Virgin, 1992)

SPILLANE, DAVY
One of the original members of Moving Hearts, Spillane has gone on to forge a solo career for himself with his imaginative – and expert – use of uilleann pipes within both a traditional

ABOVE: Davy Spillane looks heavenwards for inspiration on **Atlantic Bridge**.

and a contemporary framework. As a solo instrumentalist , Spillane remains a master of his art but his music loses a much of its impact when employed outwith the framework of a band.

Recommended listening:
Atlantic Bridge (LP) (Tara, 1987)
Pipedreams (LP) (Tara, 1991)

ST. JAMES, TONY
St. James is the alter-ego of Paul Wonderful (né Woodfull), who is also the leader of U2 celebratists The Joshua Trio. The character of Tony St. James came about following Paul's musical apprenticeship in playing with wedding bands. Peculiarly Irish – albeit

in a cabaret context – Wonderful blends his Irish bar room vocals with Las Vegas aspirations and postures to produce a comic creation par excellence. Has to be seen to be believed.

STANO
Born in 1960, and known as John Stanley to his parents, Stano is the sole Irish musician who has taken as his credo non-professional and non-academic stances. Unheard of by most outside of Ireland, Stano's deliberately improvisatory techniques have garnered him lots of critical praise but a dearth of commercial success. Generally regarded as being the instigator of electronic mass media representation within Irish rock, Stano has gone from being rigidly unorthodox (i.e., occasionally unlistenable) to almost, but not quite, embracing the mainstream (his latest band, Wreckage, go some way to bridging the gap between the avant-garde and pop). Stano is out on his own.

Recommended listening:
Content To Write In I Dine Weathercraft (LP) (Magnet, 1986)
Only (LP) (Mother, 1989)

STARJETS, THE
The most effective of the late 1970s post-punk Northern bands, the Starjets' time was brief but exhilarating. Their method of placing the Northern situation within a packed three minute pop/punk song has rarely been bettered. Following a riotously good debut album, the band broke up, with some former members going on to found The Adventurers.

Recommended listening:
God Bless The Starjets (LP) (CBS, 1979)

STARS OF HEAVEN, THE
One of many terrific Irish bands who split up before reaping their just rewards, The Stars Of Heaven were perceived to be Ireland's answer to The Byrds, Gram Parsons and The Velvet Underground in one package. Unlike others of the day (mid-1980s), the band took as blueprints American country and urban roots music. Musically, The Stars Of Heaven (Stan Erraught, guitars and lyrics, and Stephen Ryan, guitars,

and lyrics, were the musical angels) reached their apogee between 1986 and 1987, before breaking up. Shame.

Recommended listening:
Sacred Heart Hotel (LP) (Rough Trade, 1986)
Before Holyhead (EP) (Rough Trade, 1987)

STATIC ROUTINES
Band from Dundalk, County Louth, who released one sublime do-it-yourself pop single and then disappeared without trace, some members subsequently making a name for themselves in certain sectors of the Irish media.

Recommended listening:
Rock'n'Roll Clones (Single) (Good Vibrations, 1979)

STEPASIDE
Named after a Dublin suburb, Stepaside were formed in 1976 from the ashes of no-nonsense pub rock band Nightbus. Band included Deke O'Brien, the founder of Scoff records. Stepaside proved to be a highly popular pub/small venue rock band between 1977 and 1979, when their clipped brand of energetic, infectious r'n'b won over even the most cynical of customers. Fondly, if vaguely, remembered by any Irish rock music fan over 25. In the early 1980s, Deke O'Brien founded the short-lived, uncomplicated Sneeker.

STIFF LITTLE FINGERS
Undoubtedly the first commercially well-regarded Irish punk rock band, Stiff Little Fingers came to prominence in 1978 with the release of their apocalyptic debut single, 'Suspect Device'. The band were instrumental in politicising Northern Irish fear and loathing, the music barely contained, the lyrics both populist and incendiary. After a couple of years of releasing mostly excellent, essential material, the musical teeth of the band were ground down. They split up in the mid-1980s, whereupon ex-lead singer Jake Burns formed The Big Wheel to no commercial effect. Following annual reunions, SLF regrouped in the early 1990s with ex-Jam bassist Bruce Foxton replacing original member Ali McMordie, but by this time the band had outlived their

usefulness. Their early material, however, remains the most stirring and inspiring example of Northern Irish punk.

Recommended listening:
Inflammable Material (LP)
(Rough Trade, 1979)
Nobody's Heroes (LP)
(Chrysalis, 1980)
All The Best (Compilation LP)
(Chrysalis, 1983/1991)

STOCKTON'S WING

Originally a traditionally-based outfit, Stockton's Wing added electric instruments to their line-up of fiddle and mandolin in the early 1980s and haven't looked back since. Although hugely popular in Ireland and abroad for their rocked-up jigs and reels, Stockton's Wing are disliked by various rock critics for their appropriation (and dilution) of outside influences to bolster the group sound. Have now reverted to their previous acoustic-based format.

Recommended listening:
Light In The Western Sky (LP)
(Tara, 1982)
Greatest Hits Collection (LP)
(Tara, 1991)

STOKES, MARY

A respected singer of various genres, Mary Stokes and her band have been in the forefront of the resurgence of Irish-based, American-influenced blues. A good voice – although some say it's too refined for such a rough music – Mary Stokes has yet to break out of the restrictive, indigenous pub circuit. The Mary Stokes Band won the *Hot Press*/Smithwicks 1990 Award for Best Unsigned Act.

STRONG, ANDREW

The son of Irish veteran rock'n'soul singer Rob Strong, Andrew Strong was unheard of until his lead role in Alan Parker's film adaptation of Roddy Doyle's novel *The Commitments*. In that film he played the part of Deco, a gutsy young Dublin teenager with the voice of an angel roasting in hell – in other words, great in a deep throaty way. Has since signed a solo recording deal with MCA, the fruits of which will reveal whether Strong has a voice of his own and not just one for interpreting classic soul/blues songs.

Recommended listening:
The Commitments
(Soundtrack LP) (MCA, 1991)

STUMP

Formed in mid-1980s by two of the original members of Cork band Microdisney. Drummer Rob McKahey and singer Mick Lynch continued the line of Cork cacophony that began with Nun Attax. Commercially, Stump stiffed but in the land of alternative listening – where whackiness equalled wisdom – Stump ruled, albeit temporarily.

Recommended listening:
Quirk Out (LP) (Stuf, 1986)

STUNNING, THE

Formed during the late 1980s by brothers Steve and Joe Wall, Galway band The Stunning have managed to coalesce a number of styles into an appealing whole. Their combination of pop, funk, rock and acoustic ballads gives the band an all-round creative consistency. If they lack anything, it's a definitively commercial killer punch. Joe Wall has the distinction of having had a song written about his good looks by fellow County Galway band The Saw Doctors.

ABOVE: A collage of film stills on the cover of **Paradise At The Picture House**.

Recommended listening:
Paradise At The Picture House
(LP) (Solid, 1990)
Once Around The World (LP)
(Solid, 1992)

SUBTERRANEANS, THE

One of the few groups in Ireland to utilise American hip-hop rhythms and rap techniques. As such – taking

Ireland's steadfast refusal to enthusiastically and inventively embrace ethnic modes – the band are looked upon as 'interesting' rather than 'inspiring'. A good group, undervalued and overlooked because of their willingness to experiment.

ABOVE: One of Ireland's few hip-hop singles, The Subterraneans' 'Game Show'.

Recommended listening:
Game Show (Single) (Mother, 1991)

SULTANS OF PING F.C., THE

More fun and frolics from Cork, although the jokes are wearing a bit thin by now. Intermittent darlings of the music press, The Sultans have yet to prove themselves to the public at large. Their image, which appears genuine, is of whacked-out, football-loving young men. Great song titles – and they have many – don't make great songs or bands. Surprised a lot of people, including themselves, when they signed a record deal.

SWEENEY'S MEN

Formed in 1966 with core line-up of Joe Dolan (not the veteran Irish showband star), Andy Irvine and Johnny Moynihan. A year later, Dolan was replaced by Terry Woods, a versatile instrumentalist and someone who was heavily into American folk music. Perceived to be the original Irish folk rock band, Sweeney's Men swiftly attracted both public and critical attention with the release in 1968 of their eponymous debut album. Irvine left the group in 1968 to be replaced by legendary electric guitarist Henry McCullough. The band disintegrated soon after with just Woods and

Moynihan at the helm. Rightly considered to be one of the most influential of Irish folk groups, Sweeney's Men set guidelines for further electrification of previously unadulterated folk. Terry Woods is now a permanent member of The Pogues.

Recommended listening:
Sweeney's Men (LP)
(Transatlantic, 1968)
Tracks Of Sweeney (LP)
(Transatlantic, 1969)

SWIM

One of the few Irish bands to utilise the streamlined FM sound of American radio to good effect. Mysteriously, however, Swim were dropped by their record label immediately following the release of their well-received debut album – produced, incidentally, by Steely Dan's erstwhile knob-twiddler Gary Katz. Have since managed to pick up the pieces – even if lead singer Joe O'Reilly has surrounded himself with session musicians – but their long-term prospects look dubious.

*ABOVE: Swim were sunk by their record label after releasing **Sundrive Road**.*

Recommended listening:
Sundrive Road (LP) (MCA, 1990)

TASTE

The nascent Taste were formed in the mid-1960s with Rory Gallagher on guitars, Norman D'Amery on drums, and Eric Kitteringham on bass. At that time, a three-piece unit was considered both uncommon and foolhardy. By 1968, Taste personnel changed to Gallagher with Charlie McCracken (bass) and John Wilson (drums) pro-

viding the quintessential rough blues sound that was to mark out the trio as Ireland's then most attractive rock music export. By the time of the group's demise in late 1970, Taste had gained respect from their blues/supergroup contemporaries for their uncompromising, rudimentary guitar-based blues. The band also nurtured the talents of future international guitar-hero Rory Gallagher.

Recommended listening:
Taste (LP) (Polydor, 1969)
On The Boards (LP) (Polydor, 1970)

THAT PETROL EMOTION

Formed in 1984 by John O'Neill following break-up of The Undertones, That Petrol Emotion initially set out to focus on the Northern Irish 'troubles'. They released singles and a debut album that contained anti-British liner notes and questioned the presence of British troops in the six counties of the North. This agit-pop, political stance was, in the late 1980s, replaced by a more neutral sense of political awareness, yet still enveloped by their rock-hard, riff-laden pop/punk. Various record label changes in almost a decade indicate a collective resistance to compromise.

Recommended listening:
It's A Good Thing (Single)
(Demon, 1986)
Manic Pop Thrill (LP)
(Demon, 1986)
Big Decision (Single) (Polydor, 1987)
Chemicrazy (LP) (Virgin, 1990)

THEM

Them was created in 1963 by Van Morrison, a young Belfast man whose family background of blues and jazz spurred him on to a career in music. Them chose to play an eclectic mixture of American music – folk/blues, r'n'b, rock'n'roll – and injected a degree of spirited vitality to the blend . In mid-1964, Them recorded their classic tracks, 'Baby Please Don't Go' and 'Gloria', and by early 1965 had made a significant impact on the charts in both England and America. Internal, musical, financial and managerial disputes, however, proved to have too much of a negative effect on the band and, following an American tour in

mid-1966, Them split up. Although almost primordial in comparison to other 1960's artists – and even more so by today's standards – the music of Them remains inspiring and essential.

Recommended listening
Angry Young Them (LP)
(Decca, 1965)
Them Again (LP) (Decca, 1966)

THERAPY?

From Northern Ireland (Belfast), Therapy? are a three-piece hardcore band who play their gigs as if there's no tomorrow. There is, however, method behind their supposed madness. Underneath the soaring, sonic rage of their songs lies an unquestionable amount of structure and form. They might not do anything of significance in Ireland but it's a big world out there…

Recommended listening:
Babyteeth (Mini-LP) (Wiija, 1991)
Pleasure Death (Mini-LP)
(Wiija, !992)

THIN LIZZY

Indisputably Ireland's most fondly remembered rock band, Thin Lizzy were formed in 1970 by Phil Lynott, a black Irishman who effectively changed the perception of hard rock. Throughout their 13-year career, the band were able to instil a degree of lyrical sensibility and Celtic romanticism in a genre that bowed to macho posturing and chauvinism. If it was Lynott who gave the band their visual and lyrical impact, it was the band's several guitarists throughout the years

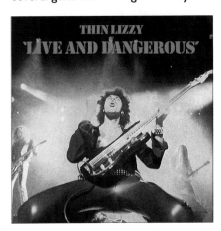

*ABOVE: **Live And Dangerous**, Thin Lizzy's classic live double album.*

(Eric Bell, Gary Moore, and latterly, the twin guitar techniques of Scott Gorham and Brian Robertson) that defined the integral Thin Lizzy sound of rock power and melody. In the latter half of the 1970s, Thin Lizzy became one of the world's best known rock bands with sell out open-air tours and keenly-anticipated albums. Although their material ranged from the thrilling to the commonplace, ultimately their recording legacy is an inspiring one. Their records are still regularly played on radio, such is their lasting popularity.

Recommended listening:
Thin Lizzy (LP) (Decca, 1971)
Shades Of A Blue Orphanage (LP) (Decca, 1972)
Vagabonds Of The Western World (LP) (Decca, 1973)
Nightlife (LP) (Vertigo, 1974)
Live And Dangerous (Live LP) (Vertigo, 1978)
Black Rose (LP) (Vertigo, 1979)
Dedicated (Compilation LP) (Vertigo, 1991)

TIBERIOUS MINNOWS

Yet another band from Northern Ireland to continue the seemingly never-ending line of well-defined and relatively pure pop music. Live, the band pack a greater punch than on record, the blending of melody and internal pop dynamics working for rather than against them. File under 'Possible Contenders'.

Recommended listening:
Time Flies (Single) (Solid, 1991)

TIR NA nOG

The partnership of Sonny Condell (see Scullion) and Leo O'Kelly within Tír Na nOg has made for some of the most intriguing and stimulating folk/acoustic rock music Ireland has ever produced. Formed at the end of the 1960s, the duo's five-year career yielded material that spanned the musical spectrum and blurred the lines between rock and folk. Well-liked by the public and respected by the critics, Tír Na nOg played singular music for unusual times. The figures of Condell and O'Kelly – both separately and together – can still be seen regularly in Irish folk circles.

Recommended listening:
Tír Na nOg (LP) (Chrysalis, 1971)
Tear And A Smile (LP) (Chrysalis, 1972)

TOASTED HERETIC

From Galway, Toasted Heretic are the surrealistic combination of a post-punk pop group and a latterday dandy. Lead singer Julian Gough is the linch-pin of the group, his eccentric ways with band and individual presentation playing a major part in their visual/media-related appeal. Musically, Toasted Heretic play undemanding, albeit cheeky and charming, fast pop.

Recommended listening:
Galway And Los Angeles (Single) (Liquid, 1991)
Another Day, Another Riot (LP) (Solid, 1992)

TOKYO OLYMPICS

Formed from the ashes of exceptional Dublin post-punk band DC Nein, Tokyo Olympics was an ill-fated excursion into a more commercial dance/ funk/soul sound. The band released one dreadful album, **Radio**, and disappeared soon after. One-time member, saxophone player Joey Cashman, is now managerially involved with The Pogues.

TON TON MACOUTE

Early-to-mid 1980s Dublin band now best known for having the precocious talents of Sinead O'Connor in their midst. Group rumoured to have flirted with aspects of voodoo, although this could be down to the obviousness of their moniker. In their time, were touted as being 'The Next Big Thing', but when O'Connor left in the mid-1980s, the band ground to an inglorious halt. The group's leading light, Columb Farrelly, now manages The Pale.

TUESDAY BLUE

Limerick band touted as definite contenders for the top, following the release of their debut single, 'Tunnel Vision', which came about after U2 bassist Adam Clayton spotted the band on television. Subsequently signed to EMI and released their debut album **Shibumi**, in 1988, amidst flurry of hype and counter-hype. Live, their performances were given extra interest by the

quasi-mystical shenanigans of lead singer Michael Ryan. Have since disbanded.

TURNER, PIERCE

Wexford man Turner gained his musical credentials with The Major Thinkers, an Irish/American power-pop/funk outfit. His acclaimed debut album was recorded in the mid-1980s with American avant-garde musician Philip Glass, and has since been superseded by subsequent releases. Turner is an oddity in Irish rock, but only inasmuch as he has a rather unique vision that is not always completely understood. His oddly beguiling music combines a Celtic sensibility with an idiosyncratic version of modern rock. Some people can't stand him, others adore him. One of Irish rock's insurgents, Turner never fails to attract comment or division.

Recommended listening:
It's Only A Long Way Across (LP) (Beggars Banquet, 1986)
Now Is Heaven (LP) (Beggars Banquet, 1991)

U2

Before 1980, U2 weren't exactly looked upon as contenders for anything. There were other Dublin-based bands who were deemed by music critics of the time to be far more capable of international success. These other bands have all disappeared and U2 are now arguably the biggest and best rock band in the world. The seeds of global domination were sown in 1976 when Larry Mullen Junior formed the band. At that time U2 were a mess both in style and content. It was with their early recorded material, however, that a form of coherency took shape, resulting in **Boy**, their debut album. From **Boy** in 1980 to **Achtung Baby** in 1991, U2 have gone through a sequence of changes that have run the gamut from the personally ambiguous to the politically obvious. They have documented their lives, loves and fears on a wide ranging series of albums and by using various musical styles in a manner that befits their intelligent and artistic leanings. They've been criticised as well as revered, with lead singer Bono, in particular, severely lambasted for his occasional forays into overtly pompous verbal indulgences. Ultimately, though, U2 have proved that where there is wilful intelligence, a willingness to experiment, and a willingness to pick up on new ideas, there is great rock music. Even their most vehement critics have realised this following the back-to-basics creative triumph of **Achtung Baby**, an uncompromising album both in terms of musical attitude and lyrical content.

ABOVE: *U2's first album of the 1990s,* **Achtung Baby,** *was a masterpiece.*

Recommended listening:
Boy (LP) (Island, 1980)
Under A Blood Red Sky (LP) (Island, 1983)
The Unforgettable Fire (LP) (Island, 1984)
The Joshua Tree (LP) (Island, 1987)
Rattle And Hum (Double LP) (Island, 1988)
Achtung Baby (LP) (Island, 1991)

UNDERTONES, THE
Never has there been such a fondly regarded Northern Irish punk band. Formed in Londonderry in 1974 by Billy Doherty, The Undertones came

ABOVE: *A raw look and raw rock for The Undertones' eponymous debut album.*

to prominence through their debut single on the Belfast record label Good Vibrations. 'Teenage Kicks' was a perfect combination of adolescent pop and energetic punk, and throughout the band's career this synthesis of styles proved to be both their great success and failure. Always a critics' favourite, the band received scant commercial reward, despite having an intelligent approach to various pop modes, a marvellous pop sensibility (courtesy of brothers John and Damian O'Neill – see That Petrol Emotion) and a vocalist as angelically inclined as Feargal Sharkey. They split up in 1983, having, ironically, released their best critically received album.

Recommended listening:
The Undertones (LP) (Sire, 1979)
Hypnotised (LP) (Sire, 1980)
Positive Touch (LP) (Ardeck, 1981)
The Sin Of Pride (LP) (Ardeck, 1983)
Cher O'Bowlies (Compilation LP) (EMI, 1986)

VIPERS, THE
One of the many Dublin-based punk rock bands that flourished in the late 1970s – a band that generated a noticeable *frisson* of media excitement and enthusiasm. Such was the spirit of the times, and like many a band before and after them (typical examples include The Modernaires, The Boy Scoutz, New Versions, The Letters and The Vultures) The Vipers dissolved into obscurity shortly after their initial spark.

Recommended listening:
I've Got You (Single) (Polydor, 1978)

VIRGIN PRUNES, THE
More than any other Irish rock band, it was The Virgin Prunes who divided opinion amongst the home rock *cognoscenti*. Formed in the late 1970s, they brought a degree of avant-garde, Grand Guignol sensibility to Irish ears and eyes. Musically and visually, The Virgin Prunes were about extremes. 'How far can we take this?' seemed to be their work ethic. Their recorded output was patchy, yet always teemed with internal contradictions and outbursts. Visually, the original band were an unpleasant but enthralling mixture of Gothic horror and tribal primitivism. They were looked upon by many as

utterly pretentious and by a few as originators of startling electronic/rock dramatics. One time members Gavin Friday and Bintti have carried on as solo artists, while Mary D'Nellon, Strongman and Dave Id continued as The Prunes.

Recommended listening:
A New Form Of Beauty, Pts 1, 2, 3 (Singles) (Rough Trade, 1981)
If I Die, I Die (LP) (Rough Trade, 1982)
The Moon Looked Down And Laughed (LP) (Baby/New Rose, 1986)
Sons Find Devils (Video) (Ikon/Factory, 1986)

WALSH, AIDAN
Initially amusing but ultimately dispiriting adjunct to the more left field aspects of Irish rock music, Aidan Walsh faded into obscurity almost as quickly as he had come to prominence. Befriended by fringe rock artists such as Gavin Friday and The Golden Horde's Simon Carmody, Walsh was catapulted into public life as the ultimate Irish rock'n'roll spaced-out oddity. The joke soon wore thin, however, and Walsh has since disappeared from view.

WATERBOYS, THE
Although Scottish in origin, The Waterboys took to the Irish muse in the late 1980s with their very much traditionally-based **Fisherman's Blues** album. Lead singer and lyricist Mike Scott had been hooked by the inherent romanticism and abstract spirituality of Irish traditional music, so much so that he based himself and his band of shifting personnel in Spiddal, Co. Galway, befriending local traditional musicians

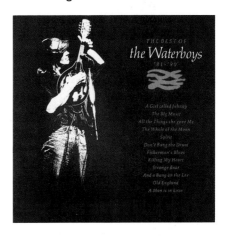

ABOVE: **The Best Of The Waterboys** *covered the years from 1981 to 1990.*

and more nationally well-known artists such as The Saw Doctors and Sharon Shannon. Scott, however, is a wandering spirit and his obsession with Irish music might decline as the years go by.

Recommended listening:
Fisherman's Blues (LP)
(Ensign, 1988)
The Best Of The Waterboys (LP)
(Ensign, 1991)

WHIPPING BOY, THE

Along with My Bloody Valentine, The Whipping Boy would appear to be Ireland's representatives in the art noise guitar band stakes. Live, their shows are the epitome of both unpredictability and unbridled excitement, and, when the band can get it together, they're unequalled. Often as not, though, they're relatively chaotic which is part of their not inconsiderable charm.

Recommended listening:
Sweet Mangled Thing
(Cassette LP only) (Gigantic, 1989)
Submarine (LP) (Liquid, 1992)

WHITE, ANDY

Since the mid-1980s, Belfast-based White has been a considerable presence on the Irish music scene, notably due to his acerbic and idiosyncratic writing style, initially modelled on 1960s Bob Dylan, but latterly all his own. White writes about matters political, be they social or sexual, but his penetrating insights are accompanied by such a degree of invective and wit that the subject matter of his songs rarely seems jaded. A man and his guitar have never sounded so essential.

Recommended listening:
Rave On Andy White (LP)
(London, 1986)
Kiss The Big Stone (LP)
(London, 1988)
Himself (LP) (Cooking Vinyl, 1990)
Out There (LP) (Warners, 1992)

WHITE, FREDDIE

Freddie White's music has been one of the main ingredients in the diet of Irish folk fans since the mid-1970s. He's entertained thousands of people with his faithful renditions of both inconspicuous and well-known American con-

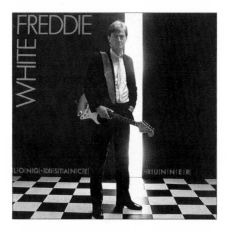

ABOVE: Freddie White, looking dapper on the cover of Long Distance Runner.

temporary songs from the pens of, amongst others, Warren Zevon, Randy Newman, Frank Zappa and Guy Clarke. Latterly, White has been writing his own material and finding that his staunch band of followers are liking it almost as much as his cover versions. A likeable performer, then, but one unlikely to crossover into the commercial mainstream.

Recommended listening:
Do You Do (LP) (Mulligan, 1981)
Long Distance Runner (LP)
(Tara, 1985)
Close To You (LP) (Lime, 1991)

WOODSBAND, THE

Developed from remnants of Gay and Terry Woods' experiences in Sweeney's Men and Steeleye Span during the early 1970s, The Woodsband continued their own delicate experimentation in the folk rock idiom. Their contribution to the form should not be overlooked, as it displayed an authoritative mixture of varying strands of folk music styles. Gay and Terry Woods went on to record albums in their own right up to the late 1970s, whereupon they parted, Gay to form Auto Da Fe and Terry to consequently join The Pogues.

Recommended listening:
The Woodsband (LP) (Decca, 1971)
Backwoods (LP) (Polydor, 1975)
Tenderhooks (LP – as 'Gay and Terry Woods') (Mulligan, 1978)

WOULD BE'S, THE

Began the 1990s with an all-time Irish classic pop song, 'I'm Hardly Ever

Wrong'. From Kingscourt, County Cavan, this sextet soon stamped their presence on both the Irish and British independent charts, but failed to capitalise on their initial media hyperbole and status as one of the best unsigned bands in the country. Came back from the doldrums in late 1991 with a new female lead singer and another single – 'My Radio Sounds Different In The Dark' – that proved their songwriting abilities, at least, had not deserted them. Undoubtedly ones to watch, but they'd better be quick...

ABOVE: A faceful of fruit on the cover of Silly Songs For Cynical People.

Recommended listening:
Silly Songs For Cynical People
(Mini-LP) (Decoy, 1991)

ZEBRA

Ireland's first and, to date, only, roots reggae group. An oddity in Irish terms, Zebra were racially harmonious, musically together, and attracted a mixed punk/roots audience. Lead singer Pete Deane went on to form one of Ireland's most criminally underrated loose funk groups, Some Kind Of Wonderful.

ZRAZY

Another curiosity in Irish terms, Zrazy are a late night, cocktail lounge type soul outfit. Funk and it's several derivatives have never rested easy within Irish bands and, while Zrazy have the necessary qualifications to transfer their own brand of loose-limbed funk'n'soul to an eager audience, finding listeners in Ireland is something the band might not be able to do. Britain, or Europe, then may be their next port of call.

INDEX

Please note that entries in italics refer to captions.